The Researcher's Toolkit

This book presents a fresh, jargon-free guide to small scale research for the beginner. *The Researcher's Toolkit* assumes no prior knowledge, and is packed with worked examples and useful tips to aid understanding and enable readers to apply the basic principles of research. Written by an experienced team of practising researchers, it covers the entire research process including: designing and framing research questions; reviewing research literature; planning research; developing a research strategy; using research instruments; analysing data and reporting the research.

This book covers statistical analysis of data and the access to and use of sensitive data. *The Researcher's Toolkit* demystifies and clearly explains the practical relevance of theory. As a guide it will appeal to a broad range of readers from undergraduates to work-based researchers, particularly those involved in teacher training, education, social work, nursing, criminal justice and community work.

Dr David Wilkinson is Research Fellow within the Higher Education Policy Unit at the University of Leeds. He has been a researcher for a number of years, and previously worked with the National Foundation for Educational Research, the University of Cambridge and City University, London.

The Contributors: Margaret Scanlon, Peter Birmingham, Dianne Hinds, Lesley Gray, Christine Gough, Jane Lovey.

The
Researcher's
Toolkit

The Complete Guide
♦ to Practitioner Research

Edited by

David Wilkinson

First published 2000 by
RoutledgeFalmer
11 New Fetter Lane, London
EC4P 4EE

Simultaneously published in the
USA and Canada
by RoutledgeFalmer
29 West 35th Street, New York,
NY 10001

Reprinted 2003

*RoutledgeFalmer is an imprint
of the Taylor & Francis Group*

© 2000 David Wilkinson for
selection and editorial matter;
individual contributors, their
contribution

Typeset in Sabon by Keystroke,
Jacaranda Lodge,
Wolverhampton
Printed and bound in Great
Britain by TJ International Ltd,
Padstow, Cornwall

*British Library Cataloguing in
Publication Data*
A catalogue record for this book
is available from the British
Library

*Library of Congress Cataloging
in Publication Data*
A catalog record for this book
has been requested

ISBN 0–415–21566–8

This book is dedicated to the memory of Margaret (Dolly) Tranter.

Contents

3 Reviewing the literature 25
PETER BIRMINGHAM

4 Research instruments 41
DIANNE HINDS

5 Finding and locating information 55
LESLEY GRAY

6 Analysing data 77
DAVID WILKINSON

Figures

List of contributors

Peter Birmingham is at the Department of Educational Studies, University of Oxford. He has been a contract researcher for a number of years and has worked with colleagues at Loughborough University and the National Foundation for Educational Research (NFER). Peter is currently exploring the use of Information and Communications Technology (ICT) in learning environments, which is part of a major project sponsored by Intel.

Christine Gough is a researcher at the Policy Research Institute at Leeds Metropolitan University. She is experienced in a wide range of approaches to research and is currently engaged in local government policy research.

Lesley Gray is with the University of Cambridge Library. She has assisted many research projects in finding and accessing information on a wide range of subjects.

Dianne Hinds is currently working with the Institute of Health and Community Studies at Bournemouth University exploring issues related to teaching and learning in the medical professions. She has been a freelance consultant for a number of years.

Jane Lovey is a researcher at the School of Education, University of Cambridge. She has worked on a number of education-related projects and is currently the head researcher on an ESCR project examining pupils with attention and activity problems.

Margaret Scanlon is currently a researcher at the University of London. She has had a number of years experience working on education-related projects at the Institute of Education, University of London and the National Foundation for Educational Research (NFER). She has been involved with national projects and has worked for a variety of sponsors including the Local Government Association, the Department for Education and Employment and the Teacher Training Agency.

Dr David Wilkinson is Research Fellow at the Higher Education Policy Unit of the University of Leeds.

Foreword

Research is not an activity particular to one discipline. My own background is broadly in the educational field, but I hope it is informed and enhanced by my own beliefs and experiences. Drawing on this facilitates a move away from the traditional image of all, or most, research texts being written by educationalists. What is an educationalist anyway? If it is someone who professes to know all about education, how education works, can string long words together in a sentence and talk about the essence of research – then that's not me and I'm definitely **not** an educationalist. What I tend to do is return to the question of the research – what is it for and what are you trying to do or find out?

The brief of this book is to be user-friendly and avoid jargon. It is not intended for academics who can quiz and argue with everything we write (or critically evaluate, as they like to call it). It is written for those new to research who need a quick fix on methods to use to help get them on their way. There should be no mystery about research; it's just like any other job really. If you're a nurse, for example, and a patient's blood pressure has dropped, you examine why this might be. It could be because the patient's diet is unsuitable, but you won't find that out unless you look into the situation and examine various data; you're already a researcher. Do you feel special now? It never ceases to amaze me how differently people treat you when you tell them you're a researcher. You appear to have special powers over everyone else; what you say, the knowledge you have is immense. I can barely recognise myself sometimes!

I am grateful to the contributors of this text for providing a broad and knowledgeable background to research in its many forms.

In Chapter 1 Margaret Scanlon covers the notion of research and its development over recent years. Chapter 2 outlines the planning processes crucial for the smooth running of a research project. In Chapter 3, Peter Birmingham provides an informative and useful guide to the literature review process.

Chapter 4, by Di Hinds, details the many research instruments that are available to facilitate the collection of data. Lesley Gray covers accessing the vast amount of data that is available through libraries in Chapter 5.

Analysing the data you have collected is covered in Chapter 6 where the different types of data are discussed and the methods used to analyse them are presented. Christine Gough provides, in Chapter 7, concise and thoughtful advice on the writing-up element of the research project.

Finally, Jane Lovey presents the story of a number of research projects – drawing on her considerable experience of conducting research in schools.

David Wilkinson

Chapter 1

Issues in research

♦ Margaret Scanlon

Research is best conceived as the process of arriving at dependable solutions to problems through the planned and systematic collection, analysis, and interpretation of data. It is a most important tool for advancing knowledge, for promoting progress, and for enabling man to relate more effectively to his environment, to accomplish his purposes, and to resolve his conflicts

(Mouly 1978: 12)

Research: what's it got to do with me?

Research is going on all around us, everyday. Most of us will at some stage participate, or at least be asked to participate, in some form of enquiry. We have all received questionnaires in the post asking about

1

our preferred brand of toothpaste, chocolate or other consumer goods. A political pollster may have approached you in the street or come to your house to find out which party you plan to vote for in the next election. If you attended a training course in the last few years it is quite likely that you will have been asked to fill out an evaluation questionnaire at the end. Certain occupational or social groups are also popular targets for researchers, for example university students.

Participating in research is normally optional, though there are some forms of information-gathering in which we are obliged to participate, including the census and the electoral register. Even if you have not participated in any form of research so far, it is quite likely that you have read about project findings in the newspapers, or seen them presented on the television news and documentary programmes. Because of the number of projects that are carried out each year, the media are highly selective about which ones they report. They tend to be either topical, 'sensational' or relevant to the particular readership of that paper. The *Guardian*, for example, is more likely to report on educational research than some of the other national newspapers because it is seen as the newspaper of teachers and lecturers. One of the most topical issues at the moment is the effects of genetically modified (GM) foods. Reports on both the scientific evidence and people's opinions on the GM issue have appeared in the media.

Research results may also have indirect effects on our lives. Policy-makers in central or local government may, for example, make decisions on the basis of research findings. Each year government departments commission universities or research organisations to carry out enquiries on their behalf. Similarly a whole range of organisations (unions, charities, local authorities) instigate studies. Even the organisations for whom we work may make changes on the basis of research that they, or others, have carried out. The connection between research and policy is explored in the following section.

What is the purpose of research?

Broadly speaking, research is carried out to fulfil one or more of the following objectives:

- To contribute to a particular discipline (for example, psychology).
- To inform policy (for example, policy on housing, crime, education).
- To address a specific issue or problem (for example, drug taking in a local school).

The objectives outlined above are not discrete or mutually exclusive: they usually overlap. For example, policy research may also contribute to disciplinary knowledge. They represent different points on a continuum rather than being completely separate. Each of these objectives is examined below. However, because this book is aimed at practitioners, the role of research in informing practice is explored in greater detail.

Contribution to a discipline

Research can be seen as enquiry designed to contribute to discipline-based knowledge. Much of what we learn in school, college or university is derived from some form of research. The social, behavioural and natural sciences, in particular, are research-based disciplines, but all subjects rely on continuous enquiry and new ideas. For example, some people may think that history is a given set of facts that do not change, but it is likely that the version of history that **we** were taught in school or university is quite different from the one which our grandparents were taught. This is partly because history is continually being revised, based on new evidence or by a re-consideration of the existing evidence. Research moves disciplines forward and is central to the life of the university.

Research that is primarily aimed at expanding theory and knowledge in a particular discipline is sometimes called 'pure' research. Pure research can be described as the 'disinterested search for knowledge and understanding for its own sake' (Robson 1993: 430). The application of findings to problem-solving in the 'real world' is not seen as a high priority and is usually left to others.

Unfortunately, although research may contribute to the knowledge base of a discipline, the findings are often accessible to only a small group. Results are usually published in academic journals that are not very user-friendly or easily accessible to the non-expert. This is why university-based research is sometimes referred to as 'research by academics for academics'. Some commentators argue that research in the social and behavioural sciences has had little influence on practice. They suggest that practitioners (for example, psychologists, teachers, nurses, etc.) do not read research findings, or if they do, they don't necessarily use them in their jobs. This apparent lack of impact of research on practice may be exaggerated; most of what these practitioners will have learned as part of their professional training will have been based on some form of research. However, once they complete their formal training, practitioners do not necessarily use the latest research to inform their practice.

Informing policy

Research may inform policy or contribute to the debate in a particular field. The increased funding for research in the 1960s, for example, was largely due to the belief that research could be used to address social and economic issues (Organisation for Economic Co-operation and Development 1995). However, the optimism of the 1960s soon gave way to disillusionment in the 1970s and 1980s when it became apparent that research had not been particularly successful in influencing policy or making the world a better place. Looking at the field of educational research, Hammersley concluded that government policy in the 1980s and early 1990s had for the most part gone against the findings of educational research (Hammersley 1993). Similarly, Adelman and Young have argued that educational research is largely ignored or taken up within political expediencies (Adelman and Young 1985). Clearly, research evidence alone is not enough to instigate change – the political will also needs to be there.

Informing practice

Concerns that conventional research was not having much impact on policy or practice led to new approaches that were seen as being more practical and relevant to 'real world' situations. In the following section I will look at two forms of real world enquiry: action research and evaluation.

ACTION RESEARCH

Action research is about diagnosing a specific problem (for example, pupil absence) in a specific setting (a school) and attempting to solve it. The ultimate objective is to improve practice in some way. Carr and Kemmis have described it in the following terms:

> Action research is simply a form of self-reflective enquiry undertaken by participants in social situations in order to improve the rationality and justice of their own practices, their understanding of these practices and the situations in which these practices are carried out.
>
> (Carr and Kemmis 1986: 162)

Action research is usually, but not always, collaborative. Teams of researchers and practitioners work together on a project. Alternatively, a project can be undertaken by the practitioners themselves, without any involvement from outside researchers. In action research, practitioners play an active role in designing the project, collecting data and implementing change. This is quite different from the forms of research described earlier where an outside researcher conducts a study (in a hospital, for example) and the role of the practitioners is usually to fill out questionnaires or participate in interviews. As McNiff has pointed out:

> Action research is an alternative to the academy-based notion that, in order to qualify as a legitimate researcher, you need to be at a university, doing research on other people (p. xiii).

Action research can take place in a diverse range of settings, for example, hospitals, companies, or schools. Observation and interviews are the two methods of data collection most often associated with action research, though a whole range of other methods, including questionnaires, tests, or documentary evidence, can also be used. The conditions imposed on other forms of research are often relaxed with action research; according to Cohen 'it interprets the scientific method much more loosely'.

Not surprisingly, action research has been criticised by those who subscribe to a more traditional scientific approach to research. Critics say that it is too subjective, it overlooks the need for systematic methods and lacks scientific rigour. Findings are not generalisable; in other words, they only apply to the environment in which the research was carried out. Therefore, people situated outside that particular environment will not learn very much from the conduct and outcome of a particular project. More detail on this form of research is provided in Chapter 4.

EVALUATION

An evaluation is a study carried out to assess the worth or usefulness of a particular service, policy or other intervention. It has a distinctive purpose, and is intended to directly inform practice or policy. Very often the evaluation will be carried out by the service provider or policy-makers themselves, or they will commission other researchers to carry out the work on their behalf. This form of research has increased in recent times partly because public services have become more accountable. Schools and hospitals, for example, are increasingly being called upon to provide concrete evidence that they are effective and providing value for money. As Robson has pointed out:

> Accountability is now a watchword in the whole range of public services involving people, such as education and health and social services. This concern in the United Kingdom arises in part from political and ideological

considerations, where it forms part of a drive to place public services within a framework similar to that governing private profit-making businesses. Similar moves in other parts of Europe, and particularly within the United States, suggest a more general phenomenon.

(Robson 1993: 171)

In order to illustrate this type of research, an evaluation of summer schools set up to improve standards of numeracy and literacy is outlined below.

Evaluation of the 1998 Summer Schools Programme

In 1997 the government instituted a programme of summer schools for 11-year-old pupils who had not reached the standard expected of their age. This summer school programme was expanded in 1998 to include over 500 Summer Literacy Schools; a pilot programme of 15 Summer Literacy Schools for pupils with special educational needs; and a pilot programme of 50 Summer Numeracy Schools.

A project was undertaken by the National Foundation for Educational Research to evaluate the success of the summer schools programme. The evaluation had three strands. Participating children were tested at the beginning and end of the summer school period to ascertain their progress in literacy or numeracy. Pupils were also asked to complete a questionnaire to judge their attitudes to their studies in literacy or numeracy at the beginning and end of the summer school period. The third element of the study was a qualitative investigation into the process of setting up and monitoring targets for the summer schools.

What is the nature of social research?

Chapter 4 describes the many data collection methods used in the social sciences. Each of these methods are different, but have certain features in common. In order to understand the nature of data collection and analysis two broad categories have been used to describe different approaches. These are: quantitative and qualitative research.

Quantitative research

Surveys, tests, structured interviews, laboratory experiments and non-participant observation are usually categorised as quantitative data collection methods. One of the important features of quantitative research is that it is highly structured and produces data which are amenable to statistical analysis. For example, structured questionnaires usually ask respondents 'to tick the appropriate box' in order to answer questions – respondents are not usually asked to say anything in their own words. They simply have to agree or disagree with statements the researcher has devised. This approach makes it easier for the researcher to quantify the data and calculate how many people made a particular point.

The results of quantitative research are presented in the form of descriptive or complex statistics, like tests of significance, correlation, regression analysis. As the name suggests, quantitative research is concerned with presenting findings in a numerical form. More detail on quantitative data analysis is provided in Chapter 6.

Qualitative research

Participant observation, unstructured interviews, or life histories are normally regarded as qualitative research methods (Bryman 1988). The resulting data is presented in the form of quotations or descriptions, though some basic statistics may also be presented.

Until the 1960s, quantitative methods and analyses dominated social research. The social sciences modelled themselves on the natural sciences, focusing on the need for objective, quantifiable information. Much of the research in psychology, for example, was based on an experimental design and carried out in laboratories or similar controlled conditions. Another important aspect of psychology research was (and still is) the use of various tests, for example, of intelligence, personality, attitude, and academic achievement. Although sociological research was not normally experimental in character, it used measurement techniques (for example, pupils ability tests) and forms of statistical analyses similar to those used in psychology. In the social sciences, surveys, tests and observation were seen as objective methods of producing 'hard' data.

This approach to research began to be questioned and challenged during the 1960s. It was argued that the application of a 'scientific' quantitative approach – in the form of surveys and experiments – failed to take into account the differences between people and the objects of the natural sciences. In the field of sociology, for example, 'radicals attacked the use of natural science methods that assumed a passive, unthinking human subject' (Shipman 1985: 11). There were concerns that the experimental method, in particular, was so artificial and removed from everyday life that the findings might not be valid; they might not represent accurately what they claim to represent. Also, many experiments were carried out using undergraduates rather than 'ordinary' people. One author criticised the typical laboratory experiment on the basis that it was 'a temporary collection of late adolescent strangers given a puzzle to solve under bizarre conditions in a limited time during their first meeting while being peered at from behind a mirror' (Tagfel 1984: 474, cit. in Robson 1993: 8). Similarly, Edgar Stones describing how educational research during the 1960s 'was concerned mainly with the development of ever more sophisticated statistical methods of measuring people' (Stones 1985: 17). Quantitative research just seemed to lack imagination.

These criticisms of quantitative research led many researchers to adapt more qualitative approaches. A qualitative research strategy, in which participant observation and unstructured interviewing were the main data collection methods, was proposed since it would allow researchers to get closer to the people they were investigating. Qualitative research in education and the social sciences developed during the 1960s and 1970s. Journals devoted to publishing qualitative research began to appear, and journals that had previously published only quantitative research started to broaden their scope (Bryman 1988: 4).

The transition from quantitative to qualitative or mixed methods was not always smooth. It was not simply a change in research techniques: it also involved change at a deeper level in terms of ideas about the nature and purpose of research (Hammersley 1993). The terms 'quantitative' and 'qualitative' are, therefore, not simply labels or categories for different research methods, but may also imply a particular outlook or concept of the nature of enquiry:

> Increasingly, the terms 'quantitative research' and 'qualitative research' came to signify much more than ways of gathering data; they came to denote divergent assumptions about the nature and purposes of research in the social sciences.
>
> (Bryman 1988: 3)

Some commentators have argued that the two approaches are basically antagonistic and should not be combined. On the other hand, writers like Bryman (1988) suggest that there is no reason why quantitative and qualitative methods should be seen as mutually exclusive. Differences exist, but the two approaches can still be used within the same investigation. There are numerous examples of how quantitative and qualitative methods have been combined in research projects, though one method is usually dominant. Furthermore, the distinction between quantitative and qualitative approaches can be rather artificial and misleading as quantitative methods, such as surveys, can produce qualitative data if open-ended questions are included. Qualitative data can also be quantified.

So far I have looked at some of the methodological debates in research. The final section in this chapter will look at research in practice, in particular the stages of research and issues for consideration before you start a project.

Stages in the Research

Research is sometimes seen as consisting of the following main stages:

- **Choosing a focus for the research**. Obviously, before you start you need a subject. If you work as a researcher or have been asked to carry out a specific project as part of your job, then your focus will already have been selected for you. One of the most challenging parts of the research may be translating the overall theme of the research into a viable project proposal.
- **Research design**. The research proposal is prepared and decisions are made regarding which methods of data collection and analysis are to be used. The research population/sample is identified.
- **Data collection**. This is the stage at which you carry out the interviews, send out the questionnaires, and so on. Not all projects involve the collection of new data; you may be analysing data already collected by someone else. This is called secondary data, whereas information gathered by the actual project team is primary data.
- **Data analysis**. This usually takes place at the end of the project when most or all of the data has been collected.
- **Writing up the results**.

In reality the stages of research are not as neatly separated as the above description might suggest. For example, you may have got to the data collection stage and found that some part of your original plan was unworkable or that there were some important issues that you had not taken into consideration in your original proposal. In which case you may have to revise some aspect of your plan. Or, you may start to analyse some parts of the data (for example, the interviews) while still collecting other forms of data. The researcher often has to move backwards and forwards between different sequences. Social research is by its very nature a messy process, as Bechhofer has pointed out: 'The research process, then, is not a clear cut sequence of procedures following a neat pattern, but a messy interaction between the conceptual and empirical world, deduction and induction occurring at the same time' (cit. in Bryman and Burgess 1994: 2). Careful planning is central to good research. For example, although data analysis is one of the last stages of a project it has to be planned at the beginning.

Some preliminary considerations

There are a number of factors that shape the way in which a project is carried out, especially the amount of time, money and other resources (for example, computer packages for the analysis of data) which are available. Accessibility of the research subjects and ethical issues also need to be kept in mind.

Resources

What researchers are able to do will depend partly on the amount of money available. Projects that are based primarily on observation and face-to-face interviews are labour intensive, and payment to researchers in the field is likely to be the largest, or at least one of the largest, costs. If the data has been collected using qualitative methods, such as open-ended interviews, then the analysis can also be very time consuming as answers will have to be coded.

Some of the main costs in survey research include: piloting the draft questionnaires, printing, posting, inputting the results and data analysis. Computer packages (such as SPSS – Statistical Package for the Social Sciences) are necessary for the analysis of most types of quantitative data, unless you have a very small sample.

Amount of time available

The time-frame in which you need to complete the research is central to your planning. Setting realistic goals is important. One trap that researchers can fall into is that they allow sufficient time to carry out the research and to analyse the data, but do not allocate enough time for writing up the final report. Unfortunately, all that hard work may come to nothing if researchers do not write up the results and share them with others.

Accessibility of research sample

Some groups are more accessible than others. Teachers, university students, and school pupils are some of the easier targets. The homeless, drug addicts or the super-rich tend to be more elusive. In some cases you may need to negotiate access with a 'gate-keeper' before you are able to reach the people you would like to reach. For example, if you want to carry out research on hospital patients, you will probably have to get the approval of the hospital management. Similarly, it is unlikely that you will be able to interview school pupils without first obtaining permission from the headteacher, and perhaps also from the children's parents. Therefore, in any one project you may have to jump several hurdles before you finally reach your sample.

In some cases negotiating access may be difficult simply because of the amount of time that the research subject would have to give to the project. For example, a headteacher might be willing to fill in a short questionnaire but might not want to participate in lengthy interviews. Guaranteeing confidentiality, arranging visits well in advance and impressing upon people the value of the research are all useful tactics in negotiating access.

Ethical issues

You may have noticed that television news programmes sometimes show pictures of 'ordinary' people to illustrate a story they are telling. For example, it could be people waiting for a train, leaving a football match or queuing up to see *Star Wars*. But are these people aware that they are being observed? Would they object if they knew they were being filmed? Should the camera crew have sought permission before filming? These are the kinds of question concerning privacy and consent that researchers need to think about. Ethical issues are, or should be, an important consideration in the design and conduct of research.

Robson (1993: 33) has identified ten questionable practices in social research. These are:

1   Involving people without their knowledge or consent.
2   Coercing them to participate.
3   Withholding information about the true nature of the research
4   Otherwise deceiving the participant.
5   Inducing them to commit acts diminishing their self-esteem.
6   Violating rights of self-determination (for example, in studies seeking to promote individual change).
7   Exposing participants to physical or mental stress.
8   Invading their privacy.
9   Withholding benefits from some participants (for example, in comparison groups).
10 Not treating participants fairly, with consideration, or with respect.

Points to note when planning your research

Resources: For example, what finance and equipment is available?
Time available: Clarify when you need to report, and plan your time accordingly.
Accessibility of sample: Are those you wish to speak to likely to want to speak to you?
Ethical issues: Show an awareness for the sensitivities of your research subjects.

Conclusion

This introductory chapter has looked at the role of research in our society. Research can contribute to disciplinary knowledge, inform policy or address specific problems. Some of the limitations of research were also discussed: very few people may see the results, or policy-makers may ignore information that does not fit their agenda.

Debates about the nature of social research were also examined. We have seen that the scientific approach has influenced social research methods but that in the last few decades qualitative methods have become more popular, particularly in sociology and education.

The chapter concluded with a brief overview of the stages in a research project and some of the factors that need to be considered before starting. It was suggested that, whilst there are different phases in research, it is by no means a linear process, moving smoothly from one point to the next. The inherent messiness of research can be reduced by careful planning. The following chapters will look in detail at the planning and conduct of practitioner research.

References and further reading

Adelman, C. and Young, M. (1985) The assumptions of educational research: the last twenty years in Great Britain. In Shipman, M. (ed.) *Educational Research: Principles, Policies and Practices*. London: Falmer Press.

Blaxter, L., Hughes, C. and Tight, M. (1996) *How to Research*. Buckingham: Open University Press.

Bryman, A. (1988) *Quality and Quantity in Social Research*. London: Unwin Hyman.

Bryman, A. and Burgess, R. E. (eds) (1994) *Analysing Qualitative Data*. London: Routledge.

Carr, W. and Kemmis, S. (1986) *Becoming Critical: Education, Knowledge and Action Research*. London: Falmer Press.

Cohen, L. and Manion, L. (1980) *Research Methods in Education* (fourth edition). London: Routledge.

Hammersley, M. (ed.) (1993) *Educational Research: Current Issues*. London: Paul Chapman in association with the Open University.

McNiff, J. (1988) *Action Research: Principles and Practice*. London: Macmillan Education.

Mouly, G. J. (1978) *Education Research: The Art and Science of Investigation*. Boston: Allyn and Bacon.

Organisation for Economic Co-operation and Development (1995) *Educational Research and Development: Trends, Issues, Challenges*. Paris: OECD.

Robson, C. (1993) *Real World Research: A Resource for Social Scientists and Practitioner-Researchers*. Oxford: Blackwell.

Sainsbury, M., Caspall, L., McDonald, A., Ravenscroft, L. and Schagen, I. (1999) *Evaluation of the 1998 Summer Schools Programme*. Slough: NFER.

Scott, D. (1996) Methods and data in educational research. In D. Scott and R. Usher (eds) *Understanding Educational Research*. London: Routledge.

Shipman, M. (1985) Developments in educational research. In Shipman, M. (ed.) *Educational Research: Principles, Policies and Practices*. London: Falmer Press.

Stones, E. (1985) The development of the British Educational Research Association: a personal view. In Shipman, M. (ed.) *Educational Research: Principles, Policies and Practices*. London: Falmer Press.

Planning the research

♦ David Wilkinson

The importance of planning

This brief chapter outlines the importance of planning your research carefully. Subsequent chapters provide guidance on the elements of the research process. Here advice is given on how to timetable and plan these elements effectively.

Depending on the scope or subject matter of your research there are a number of stages involved. Essentially these include:

• Framing your questions.
• Exploring the literature.

- Developing a strategy.
- Collecting data.
- Analysing data.
- Drawing conclusions.
- Writing/submitting your report.

Framing your questions

Most research begins with a research question or topic. In some cases, such as a personal piece of work, you may decide on your own questions; in others, they may be given to you. In either case, with any topic or focus it may be useful to ask yourself certain questions or cover issues that clarify in your own mind the extent of your investigations.

Key questions/issues

♦ Define what you want to find out.
♦ Explain why you wish to research this topic or area.
♦ Establish why it is important for this research to be carried out (for example is the literature weak in this area? Would it be useful for practitioners to read and apply the result of your work?)
♦ What data/information exists relating to similar studies elsewhere?

This clarifying process should enable you to develop and frame the questions you'd like to set out to answer in your research. Initially you will, no doubt, have generated many questions. Some of these will be related, so you should aim to limit the questions tackled in your research to a few which are clearly formulated and distinctive. Many research projects fail due to the sheer number of questions posed and the lack of clarity they display.

Following refinement and further consideration of your research questions, you should be able to develop a written research proposal (see Figure 2.1). This document sets out the scope of your research. It details the questions you intend to answer and the tools or techniques you propose to use. It should also indicate the timescale of the project and the resources it will use. This is particularly important for commissioned research, where costs are often a crucial factor.

FIGURE 2.1 Example of a research proposal

A proposal to evaluate the new bus service for Penhope Community

Background In 1999, Parfield District Council funded a pilot bus service for the community of Penhope. The aim of the service was to enable the community of Penhope to maintain links with the wider community of Parfield. This year, Parfield Council has decided to increase the service to four buses per day.

Aim The aim of the proposed research would be to evaluate how far the service has been successful in facilitating links between the rural community of Penhope and the community of Parfield.

Evaluation methods There would be two strands to the evaluation. A report combining the strands would be submitted to the Council upon completion of the work.

Strand I – Council perspective Key personnel in Parfield District Council would be contacted and their views on the bus service sought. The following information would be collected through semi-structured interviews and documentary analysis:

- Information and views on the development of the public transport system in Parfield generally and Penhope in particular;
- Perceived external influences of the development of that system; and
- The reason(s) for developing the transport link between Parfield and the community of Penhope.

Strand II – Community perspective A questionnaire survey would be developed and completed by those who use the bus service. It would be administered on the bus itself and the respondents would be offered the opportunity to complete it whilst taking their journey, or they could return it some time later (using a prepaid envelope) to the researcher. Approximately 50 questionnaires would be administered. Key question areas would be:

- Views on the cost of the journey;
- Views on the length of the journey; and
- Views on the frequency of the journey.

(continued)

FIGURE 2.1 continued

In addition, views would be sought on activities undertaken by the passengers when they reached their destination.

Timeplan The work would begin immediately and would take approximately 10 weeks to complete.

Costings
Strand I
Collecting data (6 researcher days at £180 per day)
Analysing data (3 researcher days at £180 per day)
Report writing (2 researcher days at £180 per day)
Travel/subsistence/administrative costs (£250)
TOTAL FOR STRAND I £2,230

Strand II
Collecting data (6 researcher days at £180 per day)
Analysing data (3 researcher days at £180 per day)
Report writing (3 researcher days at £180 per day)
Printing/postal costs (£300)
Travel/subsistence/administrative costs (£300)

TOTAL FOR STRAND II £2,760

TOTAL COST FOR BOTH STRANDS £4,990

Commissioned research

The vast majority of research is now sponsored research, commissioned with explicit aims and outcomes. Typically, the content of such research exercises is set out in the research specification, which may require that those undertaking the research do so using certain research tools or techniques. A research specification may be along the lines shown in the box on p. 19.

Before developing a proposal it may be useful to consult a colleague who knows about the subject of your research, or who at least is aware of it. They usually provide a helpful 'bouncing-off' point for your ideas.

Lifelong Learning in Bradfax LEA

Bradfax LEA in its aim to introduce a comprehensive Lifelong Learning Programme wishes to commission a consultant/research body, with experience of post-compulsory education, to carry out an audit of its Adult Learning provision in order to assist the development of the LEA's Lifelong Learning Programme.

Interested parties should submit a proposal detailing how they intend to audit the Adult Learning provision, and quote the fee required within a budget of £12,000. It is anticipated that the work will be carried out during the month of July, and a final report submitted to the Chief Education Officer by 1st September.

Exploring the literature

In many proposals, the research makes reference to key literature to emphasise points and provide authority to the work being undertaken. Therefore, early consultation of the literature in a research project is important. Chapter 3 details the processes involved in comprehensively reviewing the literature and this should be carefully timetabled into the project. A quick literature search or scan through relevant journal abstracts in the early stages of the research should, however, provide assistance in establishing the key concerns in your subject area. Following a comprehensive literature review, you may find that your original research questions are no longer appropriate or require reshaping (for example, you may discover that very similar work has been carried out elsewhere). In this case you would need to refine your questions to concentrate on an area not explored fully in the other work, or concentrate on questions which add to the research already conducted. This re-forming of the research is quite common and you should not feel obliged to stick rigidly to your original questions. I have known many substantial projects change their focus once it has emerged that similar work has either been carried out or is being carried out elsewhere.

Developing a strategy

Once you have framed and perhaps reshaped your questions, how will you actually go about answering them? You will need to develop a strategy for your research. The example research proposal (Figure 2.1) indicates the strategy or methods used to fulfil the requirements of the research. It indicates the tools, techniques and instruments needed to collect and analyse the data. Your research strategy should focus on the questions and explore the most effective and efficient ways of answering these questions. For example, your strategy should detail which research instruments you will use and how you will collect the data (through documentary analysis, via telephone/face-to-face interviews, through questionnaires, by using case studies, etc.). The strategy forms a major part of the research and it is useful to develop a visual plan (see Figure 2.2) as part of the strategy indicating key milestones in the research.

Of course, even the most carefully organised research may not go according to plan. For example, it might prove difficult to interview teachers during the summer holiday when the school is closed! Therefore, you need to build into your plan some 'leeway' and you may need to change the order of things slightly. Attempt to view your plan as a template: all the necessary ingredients for the

---

Week 1 to 2
- Develop questions
- Consult colleagues
- Refer to key journals
- Review current research in the area
- Write proposal

Week 3 to 10
- Develop strategy for research
- Design instruments
- Pilot instruments
- Refine instruments
- Select sample group
- Administer instruments

Week 10 to 13
- Collate data
- Analyse data
- Submit draft report to colleagues for comment

Week 14
- Submit report

FIGURE 2.2 Example research plan

research should be there, but the ordering of them may change. This shouldn't alter greatly the eventual 'dish' that you serve.

Collecting and analysing data

Do not underestimate the length of time it takes to collect data. In addition, do not overestimate the amount of data your are likely to be able to collect. Many researchers expect to achieve a response rate of between 30 per cent to 60 per cent for questionnaires. Therefore, do not be too disheartened if, after all your work, only 30 out of 100 questionnaires are returned. You should, however, anticipate that this might be the case and you should aim to distribute many more questionnaires (subject to cost considerations) than you expect to be returned completed.

The ease of analysing your data will depend on how well structured your instruments for collecting the data are. Chapter 4 details the design of research instruments – one of the most common being the questionnaire. (See Figure 2.3 for an example plan of a questionnaire survey.) Many researchers rush to use this instrument as they often view it as a cheap and easy way to collect data. In many cases this is true, but the structuring, planning and layout of a questionnaire all require careful consideration, which is often a time-consuming process.

The process of analysing data can also take time and it may even produce results you did not expect to find. Again, be prepared for this and apportion time to consider the implications of the data being different to how you expected them to be. Can you explain this? Does it necessitate further analysis or data collection?

Drawing conclusions

Drawing conclusions from your data is often the most difficult part of a research project. You may have considered your conclusions when designing or framing your research questions. Once you have collected your data you must ask yourself how the data answers your original questions. Does it provide evidence (in your findings) upon which to make conclusions? Do you consider alternative explanations for your conclusions? In other words, is your research topic subject to other factors perhaps not considered in your work? It is not a major failing if you indicate that other work or external factors beyond the remit of your research affect your conclusions. However, it would be a failing if you didn't mention them. In addition, do you indicate the strengths and weaknesses of your research (or methodological) approach? These are the types of question you should seek to address in the conclusions of your research report. They show that you have evaluated the approach you have taken in the work.

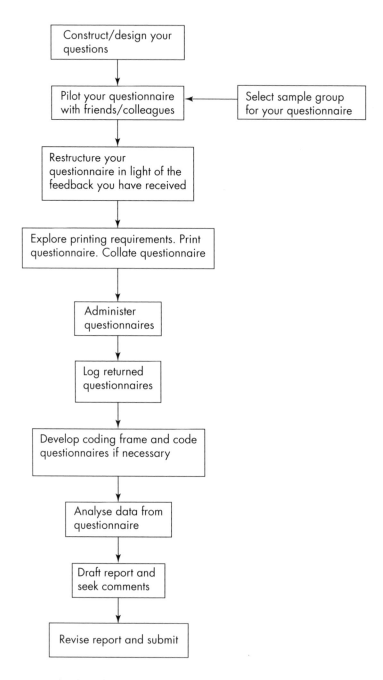

FIGURE 2.3 Example plan of a questionnaire survey

Writing and submitting your report

In PhD research, which takes an average period of three years full-time study, it is usual for 6 months to be given to the write-up of the work. This is often in addition to notes and draft chapters written throughout the period of study. Many of those new to research don't allow enough time for writing. The process often involves drafting and re-drafting. In, say a 10-week project you should aim to leave perhaps 2 weeks for writing the report. Chapter 7 provides further detail on the writing-up process.

References and further reading

Blaxter, L., Hughes, C. and Tight, M. (1997) *How to Research*. Buckingham: Open University Press.

Herbert, M. (1990) *Planning a Research Project: A Guide for Practitioners and Trainers in the Helping Professions*. London: Cassell.

Chapter 3

Reviewing the literature

♦ Peter Birmingham

The purpose of carrying out a literature review

Everyone who decides to undertake a piece of research should feel confident and knowledgeable about the topic they are studying and the questions they are asking. A researcher who fails to invest sufficient time and effort into investigating others' previous, related work in their chosen area of study will be unable to make much progress. How can you refine and build upon the work of those who have come before if you are not fully aware of the efforts they have made and the conclusions at which they have arrived? Likewise, once you have decided to undertake a piece of research you should want your finished work to be both *valued* and *valuable*. It will be most highly valued if it is apparent that it has been informed by, and has expanded upon, a rigorous and thorough attention to similar work undertaken in the past. It will be valuable if, precisely because of the efforts devoted to its formative stages, the research reveals the final pieces of a complex puzzle, or indeed introduces more puzzles to the debate.

To put it simply, you cannot advance knowledge in your field without first learning what has been achieved by others and what still remains to be achieved. The literature review is to a research project what the foundations are to a house. Without solid foundations the house is likely to fall down, and without a detailed look at the literature, your project is likely to be simplistic, naïve and an inferior repetition of work already completed by someone else.

Learning to review the literature has never really received the attention it undoubtedly deserves. Despite the long-standing tradition of literature reviews featuring in the early stages of research, there has been a significant lack of attention paid to just how a researcher ought to go about searching for, collecting, evaluating and using past research in his or her current project. In fact, it seems to be a lot more difficult to provide a definition of a literature review that we can all have confidence in than it is to recognise one on paper when we turn to the first few pages of a research report.

Researchers' opinions of, and attitudes to, the nature, process and purpose of a literature review vary enormously. There are, however, common elements that all researchers ought to take on board. Why do we review the literature?

Why carry out a literature review?

A literature review:
♦ reports the research of others and not the new research itself;
♦ provides a background to the new research;
♦ provides a peg on which to hang the new research;
♦ links the new research to what has preceded it;
♦ identifies effective practice;
♦ justifies the need to conduct new research;
♦ provides a bibliography;
♦ seeks to do one or more of the following:
  (a) describe;
  (b) summarise;
  (c) interpret;
  (d) synthesise;
  (e) evaluate;
  (f) clarify;
  (g) extend;
  (h) integrate others' research.

A literature review enables a researcher to accomplish a number of more specific aims. It is likely, for example, that in the early stages of your research you may have only a vague idea of the area you would like to explore more fully. You may have only a tentative outline of your research problem. This should not give you cause for concern. A review of the literature will help you to focus your tentative problem by both limiting and defining more clearly the topic you are interested in researching. Look out for recommendations made by researchers for those intent on continuing with research in a particular field. You may be provided with advance warnings of possible pitfalls, or research questions that have been thus far neglected. Reading around the subject will help you to distil the issues you wish to concentrate upon and leave you with a concise, detailed and distinct plan of action.

The existing literature relating to the topic you wish to study is just as important for what it omits as it is for what it contains. Do not be overwhelmed by the work others have done before you. You may have experienced something related to your area of interest that others have not; an experience that allows you to approach the problem from a unique and novel perspective.

In examining the available literature it is tempting to look first (or only) at the results and conclusions the authors have drawn. It is advisable to employ a little scrutiny. Rather than focus on results alone, look at the methods, measurements and subjects that the researcher has used. In tackling a particular research problem, the use of certain methodologies and sampling procedures will prove more fruitful than the use of other, less appropriate strategies, and a good researcher will justify his or her choice from a range of possible options. Do not disregard whole studies because you may not be convinced by their results. If you throw out the baby with the bath water you may miss out on insights into how best to design a piece of your own research that produces findings which stand up to the criticism and scrutiny of others.

Having discussed why a literature review is a vitally important element of any research, it is appropriate to consider just what such a review might entail. It seems that there are as many approaches to undertaking a literature review as there are research methods textbooks available to new researchers keen to conduct their own inquiries. It is fair to say that experienced and novice researchers alike differ in their understandings of literature reviews because of this. But just what are these understandings? A study of 41 research students engaged in higher degrees at an Australian university concluded that they had six qualitatively different conceptions of the literature review (Bruce 1994: 221–3):

1   A list or collection of descriptions and key words from journal articles, books, newspapers, etc. that represent the available literature on the research topic. The emphasis is on the listing of the literature rather than its content.

2	The act of searching for and identifying information of relevance to the research topic. Again, the content of the literature does not receive priority. Instead, the literature's ability to steer the researcher in the direction of other, relevant existing literature is the prime motivation.

3	A survey or a scan of past, present and possible future writing or research related to the research topic. The focus is very much on the content of the literature, especially what is known about a particular topic.

4	A means by which a researcher can increase his or her knowledge of a particular research topic and test his or her own thoughts or hypotheses. The focus here is on the literature's potential to influence the *researcher*, in terms of his or her personal development, but not to influence the *research*.

5	An instrument capable of supporting, influencing, directing, shaping or changing the research to be undertaken. In this conception the literature influences both the researcher and the research.

6	A report in its own right, or as a discrete section of a larger report, in which the researcher frames and thematically organises the literature. It is a final representation of the ways in which the literature has impacted upon both the researcher and the research project.

Definitions of literature review

- A list
- A search
- A survey
- A knowledge enhancer
- A supporting/directing tool
- A report

(adapted from Bruce 1994: 221–3)

Bruce notes that there is a relationship between the six conceptions. She describes them as 'progressively more encompassing' (Bruce 1994: 225). It is a good idea to view the conceptions as six rungs of a ladder. It is not possible to climb on to a higher rung without first being familiar with, and actually using, the lower rungs. Similarly, you continue to appreciate the lower rungs in assisting you to climb higher, long after you have reached the top of the ladder.

Locating the literature

Wherever you go or to whomever you speak in order to gather your information, the first thing you ought to do is identify and list as many key words as you can that relate to the topic of your research. This is because, as a general rule, all resources open to you – apart from people with experience or knowledge related to your topic you might be lucky enough to access – are organised by subject. It is by means of these key words that you will be able to find information connected with the topic you intend to study. They provide you with a starting point. Of course, in these very early stages of your research you will not want to overlook related studies completed by others before you, especially those which may prove to be important or relevant. You should therefore 'cast your nets' as widely as possible when you come to making a note of key words.

Try thinking of a way to turn the topic of your research into a question. What is it you may wish to find out? If, rather than doing the research yourself, you were able to approach someone in your imagination and ask them to give you the answers you seek, how would you phrase the question? For example, if you were a nurse interested in investigating the ways in which elderly patients on geriatric wards were viewed by your colleagues, you may ask: 'What are the attitudes of medical professionals towards geriatric patients in hospital?' Alternatively, as a teacher (say, of history) you may be interested in looking at how a new computer program may impact upon a lesson. In this case you might ask: 'What effect do computers have on the teaching of history?' In both cases you can see that some of the words within your question would be appropriate key words with which to start your search: ATTITUDES, MEDICAL PROFESSION, GERIATRIC, PATIENT, HOSPITAL, and COMPUTERS, TEACHING, HISTORY.

This initial list of key words may be very short – as in the second example above which contains only three words – but do not be put off by this. The next stage is to take each of the words from your list in turn and think of related words or phrases. You might use a thesaurus to help you find these synonyms. Terms related to COMPUTERS, TEACHING and HISTORY which you think appropriate to add might include INFORMATION TECHNOLOGY, IT, ICT, ILT, PEDAGOGY, CLASSROOMS, TEACHER TRAINING, HUMANITIES, and so on. Soon your list will have grown, along with your chances of finding as much of the literature as possible when you begin your search.

The information you do find might be located in a range of different sources, two of the most common being books and journals. Your first port of call should therefore be a library. This may be your local municipal library, a college or university library you may be a member of, or a specialist library that houses literature and information on topics relating to your job or profession. The range of materials which you may be able to access will no doubt vary according to your own particular circumstances, and you should make efforts to find out what facilities are available to you. After all, you want to maximise your chances of collecting as much information relating to your research topic as you possibly can. The more libraries you can visit and the wider and more specialist the content held in them, the more chance you have of your literature review being thorough and exhaustive.

The library catalogue will tell you which books are held there. The catalogue may take the form of a traditional card catalogue, a microfiche, or – as is increasingly common – a computerised version often referred to as OPAC. Although the computerised version will let you use a variety of search options (including author, year of publication, ISBN), *all* catalogues, in whatever form, are searchable by subject. By comparing the list of key words you have compiled with the list of subjects found in the library catalogue you ought to be able to find books that may prove a good resource for your own research. Obviously, some books will be more relevant than others, and the catalogue can only ever point you to the books that that particular library has on its shelves.

There will, of course, be more books written about a particular subject than any single library can ever hope to stock. It is important, therefore, to consult some general *bibliographical* sources. Bibliographies should be available for you to consult in most types of library, and include details on what is, or has been, in print related to your area of interest. The *British National Bibliography* and the *American Book Publishing Record* include references by author, title or subject to books published in the UK and the United States respectively. *Whitaker's Books in Print* may also be of use to you, although this bibliography tends to be organised mainly by author or title. As you consult these resources you may see patterns emerge. Perhaps a small number of authors appear again and again, or you may notice alternative synonyms to those you listed crop up repeatedly. In either case, cross-referencing the bibliographies with the actual library catalogue may help you to find more books of relevance to your topic of study than you thought were available after consulting just the library catalogue.

It is only a matter of time before a book, once published, becomes out of date. Any new developments in the subject covered by a specific book will go unmentioned until (or unless) a subsequent edition is published. Journals, on the other hand, are published at regular intervals throughout the year, and each new number contains the most up-to-date information available on a particular topic along with information that is often unsuitable to publish in book form, for example debates and correspondences, book reviews and editorial comments. You would find it an inefficient use of your time to look through the contents of numbers and volumes of journals devoted to the topic that interests you to find potentially useful information. Instead, you ought to use *indexes* and *abstracts*, which are intended to help you identify and locate research articles and other information relevant to your own project. Finding precisely what you want is by no means a straightforward task, but to discover a reference closely centred on exactly the nature of your own inquiries has the potential to be the most valuable single find in your entire investigation, so persevere!

For more detail on accessing information, particularly through a library, see Chapter 5.

Selecting appropriate literature and maintaining literature notes

As you begin your investigations in earnest you will begin to get a feeling for the amount of information that has been written by others about the topic you wish to research. You might find yourself with tens or possibly hundreds of pieces of relevant information each of a different length, prospective audience or focus of study. At this point you need to consider ways in which you might manage and organise all this information to prevent it getting out of hand. A good idea would be to produce concise summaries of the book chapters and journal articles you have collected on small record cards, but this will prove an effective and helpful way to summarise all the information only if you are consistent in your selection of the material to be extracted.

Begin with the most recent studies. They are likely to be more valuable to you as their authors should have used earlier research as a foundation. Apart from noting accurately where to find the material again once you have returned it to the shelf, a good summary of a piece of research literature you uncover should include details about:

- The problem the material is attempting to address.
- The purpose(s) of the study or studies related in the material.
- Brief information about the population(s) studied – comprising whom? How many subjects?
- Methods and techniques used by the researcher(s).
- The results of the study or studies.
- Any conclusions.

Introductions to articles usually contain details on the first two of the above points, while more information on methods and results is usually reported in the middle and the end of articles respectively. Of course, after reading through the abstract at the beginning or the summary at the end, you may decide that a particular article contains insufficient information relevant to your study to justify reading the whole thing from end to end. When you do find the articles you think could be of benefit to your own research you shouldn't find it too difficult or time-consuming to abstract these and any other details you consider especially important.

One thing is certain: the contents of a research article or chapter of a book will remain fresh in your mind only for the time you are reading it. With so much to familiarise yourself with you will begin to confuse the contents and conclusions of others' research very early on in your reading. With each new piece of literature you consult you will find yourself relying more and more on the summaries you make, so it is worth investing some time and effort in collating thorough and consistent notes at this stage.

Apart from listing all the pertinent points in each of the studies you consider to be important, you might like to record your own evaluation of the study at the same time. In your opinion, does it contain any particular strengths or weaknesses, perhaps relating to the techniques employed in the study, unfamiliar or unusual methods to collect or analyse data, or interesting theoretical underpinnings? Most importantly, how might the article you have just read relate to the work you are keen to undertake? How significant is the material for your own research?

You should attempt something similar with articles or book chapters which, rather than reporting instances of actual research, comprise essays, discussions, debates, opinions or syntheses of past research connected in some way with the work you wish to undertake. One way to familiarise yourself quickly with this type of material might be to scan what has been written by reading the first one or two sentences of each paragraph. This ought to provide you with enough information to help you to decide whether an article or chapter is worth reading thoroughly from start to finish. For those articles you choose not to discard you should still be able to summarise the problem being addressed in the material, and the conclusions drawn by the author, despite the less rigid, more fluid structure of book chapters. In such cases your focus should turn to summarising and evaluating the theme or themes of the material: What is the author saying? What reasoning, logic or arguments does he or she use to say it? On what is the author's reasoning and logic based? Can you see any strengths or weaknesses in the author's arguments?

Occasionally you may find an author has written something in a particularly skilful way, for example managing to phrase a complex idea, argument or conclusion in concise and clear terms. Similarly, you may sometimes come across a couple of lines in a report which sum up the essence of the whole article. If you find yourself in this situation it would do you no harm to copy this down carefully somewhere in your summary, enclosing the extract in quotation marks and noting down the relevant page number.

Aggregating literature material

As you continue with this process you will begin to find yourself surrounded by dozens of record cards each containing a summary of a piece of work related to, or important for, your own intended research. Just as it is necessary to impose some kind of order upon your choice of key words in the earliest stages of your literature search if it is to be focused and well-defined, it is equally necessary to organise and group all your record cards in order both to maximise their value for your research and to minimise your workload.

One way of organising your summaries is to code each one according to the characteristics of the information it contains. You may find that your original key words can, on the whole, act as 'pegs' on which to 'hang' your summaries. For example, the author of a review of the literature written about the use of computer software in classrooms might code each summary according to one or more of many issues which arise when bringing new technology into schools:

- L   Articles dealing with pupils' abilities and how pupils Learn.
- U   Articles about the User-friendliness of software, its scope, its aims and the way it ought to look.
- M   Articles relating to the structure and content of additional Materials, such as users' guides and teachers' notes to supplement the software.
- T   Articles dealing with Technical issues surrounding the software, such as its compatibility with a school's existing hardware.
- E   Articles about Educating pupils using software, for example, when to use it or when not to use it.
- R   Articles about the technology's impact on teacher and pupil Roles, including the interactions between pupils, teachers and computers.

By writing the appropriate code in, say, the top right-hand corner of each record, it will help you to become aware of the ways in which researchers before you have tried cogently and sensibly to make sense of all the issues which surround a topic. It will also enable you to locate more quickly all your notes relating to one area within your topic of study and, perhaps, most important for the novice researcher overwhelmed by information, it should ease the burden of writing up your review by dividing it into easy-to-handle, bite-size pieces.

Critically analysing the literature

How much trust should you place in the research you find? Even after you have discarded those studies that appeared to be pertinent to your own research but, on closer inspection, proved not to be, does each and every piece of research you are left with deserve to be a part of your own inquiry? If not, on what basis should you include and exclude material in the section of your own work which deals with related, previous research?

In short, you may have to make some *evaluative decisions*. In order to do that, you have to establish your own set of criteria for judging the *adequacy* of the material in front of you. As authors base the conclusions of their studies (at least in theory!) on the outcomes of analyses of the data they have collected, any critical evaluation ought to include as its focus a thorough scrutinisation of a study's methodology and results sections. You may find instances where data have been collected or recorded unreliably or erroneously. You may also discover that results or analyses have been calculated incorrectly, and that conclusions have been made on the basis of those miscalculations. Such errors do occur – researchers are not an infallible breed. Obviously, the extent to which you feel confident in your own ability to make calculations and re-calculations of others' data to check their reliability and authenticity will depend on your background and experience of these situations, but even the least confident of novice researchers should be able to spot intuitively any reported values or measurements that seem spurious, or at least a little odd. Can the results be trusted in your opinion? Do you think the study was carried out in a sufficiently careful manner? After considering just these few basic questions you ought to be able to do one of three things:

- **Include** the study in the literature review section of your own work.
- **Exclude** the study because it 'fell at the first fence'.
- **Reserve judgement** as to the trustworthiness of the study until you are able to make a more informed decision, perhaps based on a wider range of criteria for judging research quality.

Even at this stage you should be aware of something called *confirmatory bias*. Researchers – as well as being fallible creatures – do not live in a vacuum. We have been known to have biases and predispositions towards certain points of view and certain outcomes of studies rather than others. This, if not sufficiently borne in mind, could lead your evaluation of another's research to be coloured or distorted by its premise, outcomes or conclusions. Experiments have shown that a reviewer's predispositions towards a review's results can influence his or her judgement about the quality of a piece of research. In the past, reviewers have accepted material which, despite containing questionable and dubious methodology, has supported their own intuitions, while rejecting sound and well-grounded research that advances counter-intuitive conclusions (Mahoney 1977; Lord et al. 1979).

Related work in this area has shown that comparatively inexperienced researchers are not the only ones to succumb to these subjective pressures. Cooper

(1989) found evidence to suggest that the decisions of professional evaluators (such as those who judge submitted manuscripts for possible publication in journals) are occasionally made on the basis of where, along two dimensions, they locate a particular research paper:

- their perception as to the way in which a study to investigate a particular topic or problem should be designed; then
- their judgements as to how well, once the research is underway, it meets its own design criteria.

In other words, opinions about the trustworthiness of a piece of research may depend on answers to the questions 'is this the best way to study X?' and 'now you have decided to study X in this way, how well is your study going?' As with confirmatory bias, these judgements are based on prior opinions of how best to accomplish a piece of research so that its results are valid and stand up to scrutiny. Bearing all this in mind, and allowing yourself as much as possible not to be influenced by such biases, what means other than your own intuition do you have at your disposal to judge the adequacy of a particular study? Let the material defend itself. Try asking yourself the following questions.

Does the article go into sufficient depth?

Does it provide you with enough information about, for example, the reasons why the research was conducted; the context or location in which the research took place; the methods employed and the results obtained? Do you get the impression the author has included as much detail in the write-up as he or she was capable of, or do you feel that there have been certain omissions?

Are there any inconsistencies?

For example, are there inconsistencies in the way the author refers to, or provides information about, the size(s) of the population(s) studied? Are references to the *initial* sample and the *achieved* sample made consistently? Confusing the number of people originally contacted to partake in the research and the number who actually responded and took part will produce inaccurate results, occasionally skewed in favour of the researcher! Does the researcher inform you to your satisfaction of details about response rates, the sizes of sub-samples, the number of drop-outs and those unable to be contacted (sometimes referred to as the attrition rate), and the total on which any percentages are based?

Where did the author obtain this information?

Is it clear how and from whom information presented to the reader as fact was obtained? Which questions were asked? Of whom? Were there any attempts to obtain corroborative evidence from another source? Do you sense any assumptions made by the author? In other words, has he or she accepted some aspects of the research blindly which you would have liked to have been investigated further?

Are the author's claims reasonable?

Do you feel that too much is being claimed on the basis of the evidence in front of you? Have the author's analyses been adequate? When something is referred to as 'significant', is it? How has the author measured significance? Do you consider there to be equally plausible explanations for the results of the research that the author has failed (or worse, refused) to consider?

Example of a literature review

What follows is an excerpt from a chapter of a book by Fenton et al. (1998) which explored the relationship between the social science community and the media. The aim of the introductory chapter from which this excerpt is taken was to set the scene for the presentation of previous research findings into the portrayal of social science research in the British mass media, and how it compared with the coverage of *natural* science. This excerpt provides a neat and concise summary of research into the nature of media coverage of science.

Science in the media
It is necessary to cover the reporting of science in the mass media because most of the issues addressed in such research are replicated in studies of social science reporting. Indeed, as has just been suggested, much research on science in the media subsumes the representation of social science reporting.

A major fixation in this research is with textual representation and *accuracy*. Generally speaking, science reporting comes across as reasonably accurate and no worse than other areas of news reporting; inaccuracy often tends to involve omissions – of names of all researchers involved, of methods, of qualifications of findings – though misleading headlines, over-generalisation and misquoting seem quite common (for example, Tichenor et al., 1970; Tankard and Ryan, 1974; Pulford, 1976; Singer, 1990; Peters, 1995). In one of the most frequently cited studies, Tankard and Ryan (1974) asked scientists, whose work had been reported in newspaper articles, to specify whether the articles contained any of 42 kinds of error. A mean error rate of 6.22 was found with only 8.8 per cent of articles revealing no errors. The most common errors, that is those found in over 30 per cent of articles, were: omission of information about methods; omission of important information about results; omission of certain names within a research team; omission of qualifications to aspects of findings; and misleading headlines.

Pulford's (1976) partial replication of this research used a smaller list of 11 types of error, made up of those most frequently mentioned in the Tankard and Ryan research and of general categories which subsumed a number of the less frequently mentioned errors. Using this probably more realistic list, 29.4 per cent of articles emerged as having no errors. In this and subsequent research, the kinds of error are very similar to those discerned in Tankard and Ryan's investigation. Thus, Moore and Singletary's (1985) examination of network television news coverage of science found that complaints from scientists involved tended to revolve around inadequate air time, omission of details, sensationalism, and incorrect impressions being given. However, in spite of the criticism of inaccuracy that scientists often level at scientific articles, they tend to think more highly of articles in which they themselves are cited or quoted (Dunwoody and Scott, 1982). There is also variation between the media: Hansen and Dickinson (1992) found that scientists in Britain thought more highly of television and radio stories in which they had appeared than of newspaper ones. Moreover, they thought more highly of newspaper articles in the 'quality' press than those in the 'popular' press. The finding that television was the medium with which scientists were most pleased (very slightly more than radio) is surprising in light of Friedman's comment that it is 'perhaps the hardest medium of all for science communication' (1986: 35). Certainly, in some forms of television programme, like the audience discussion programme, the scientific expert is especially vulnerable to ridicule and to an inability to get his or her point across (Livingstone and Lunt, 1994; Ussher, 1994).

The problems of accuracy tend to be attributed to the different norms and cultures of news-gathering organisations and of science (predominantly in universities, but also in government). Writers on science in the media typically draw attention to such things as the deadlines to which journalists have to work and the competition for newspaper space or air time in which they have to engage. Journalists often do not have enough time to assimilate fully the information they are given and have to write quickly. In the process, important details from the point of view of the scientist may be omitted. The pressure for space or air time means that the journalist has to write a piece that will attract the attention of editors, many of whom are not particularly attracted to scientific stories. Consequently, scientific stories have to be engaging and this means that certain details which might detract from, or at least not contribute to, their allure are likely to be ignored. This position is nicely captured in a comment from a science reporter quoted by Winsten:

> I'm in competition with literally hundreds of stories every day, political and economic stories of compelling interest . . . We have to almost overstate, we have to come as close as we can within the boundaries of the truth to a dramatic, compelling statement. A weak statement will go no place.

> (1985: 9)

Moreover, writers frequently draw attention to the fact that editors will often make substantial changes to a journalist's piece in order to enhance its interest. A further source of inaccuracies that is often mentioned by writers is the almost inevitable problem of translating complex ideas into generally readable prose.

Nelkin (1987) argues that most science reporting is remarkably homogeneous. It tends to conform to a 'frame' which acts as a template. As a result, certain images, motifs and concerns seem to run through a wide variety of writings regardless of the topic itself. Scientists tend to be depicted in heroic terms, selflessly furthering knowledge for the nation and for humanity. The imagery of science (laboratories, test-tubes, the technology of science) tends to replace actual content. Science also tends to be depicted as a series of vital dramatic events, which often leads to the charge of sensationalism from scientists themselves. This concentration on break-throughs and major discoveries is indicative of another feature of science reporting – a focus on competition between research teams. Moreover, in spite of the focus on the heroic scientist, science reporting tends to be depopulated. There tends to be little attention given to the actual procedures of science (other than iconically). In a study of the Canadian press, Einsiedel (1992) found that only a quarter of stories contained details about procedures. As a result, the scientific labour process tends to be sidelined. In an examination of the British scientific television news magazine, *Tomorrow's World*, Murrell (1987) found that the work of scientists, their personal goals and the conflicts that are rife in the scientific community are ignored. This contrasts sharply with other spheres of news reporting, such as sport, in which there is a great deal of interest in the world and lives of sporting personalities.

This template for science writing reflects the notions of what constitutes news and how it should be presented among journalists in general (Hansen, 1994). In a study of scientific journalism in German periodicals, Böhme-Dürr

(1992) found that journalists' main reasons for choosing a story were timeliness, perceived reader interest and informativeness. These factors presumably lie behind the well-documented tendency for medicine and health-related topics to predominate in what actually does get published (Jones et al., 1978; Dennis and McCartney, 1979; Einsiedel, 1992; Hansen and Dickinson, 1992; Hansen, 1994).

Science journalists carry around a clear notion of source credibility, based largely on cues such as seniority and affiliation; they tend to use the same sources again and again and deliberately create a feeling of mutual trust. Writing mainly about the USA, Nelkin (1987) notes that science journalists cultivate relationships with scientists and rely on what she calls a 'stable' of reliable figures. Hansen writes of Britain that most science journalists 'have built up a mental map . . . of who does what and where in Britain' (1994: 119). Particularly in the so-called 'quality press', science journalists build up relationships of trust with sources and go to great pains to get their information right in order not to jeopardise those relationships. Such findings have prompted some writers to describe the relationship between sources who are scientists and science journalists as 'symbiotic' (Peters, 1995: 43), though not all writers agree with such a view (especially Dunwoody, 1986a). In Norway, a country that does not have a tradition of specialist science journalism, 'journalists seem to prefer sources who can provide clear-cut findings and express clear-cut points of view' (Eide and Ottosen, 1994: 428); they also report a harmonious relationship between the media and academics. As a body, scientists are probably not highly regarded by journalists. According to Böhme-Dürr, journalists on German magazines perceive scientists as 'supercilious, uncooperative, manipulative, and conceited' (1992: 171). However, this makes it all the more necessary for journalists to nurture relationships with scientists who can fulfil their requirements.

A higher proportion of articles than might be supposed are source initiated, that is, they are set in train by scientists themselves. In both Norway and the UK around 25 per cent of articles are generated in this way (Hansen and Dickinson, 1992; Eide and Ottosen, 1994). This suggests that scientists can be more proactive than might generally be appreciated.

(Fenton et al. 13–16)

References and further reading

Bruce, C. (1994) Research students' early experiences of the dissertation literature review. *Studies in Higher Education*, 19(2): 217–29.

Cooper, H. M. (1989) *Integrating Research: A Guide for Literature Reviews*. London: Sage.

Fenton, N., Bryman, A., Deacon, D. with Birmingham, P. (1998). *Mediating Social Science*. London: Sage.

Lord, C., Ross, L. and Lepper, M. (1979). Biased assimilation and attitude polarization: the effects of prior theories on subsequently considered evidence. *Journal of Personality and Social Psychology*, 37: 2098–109.

Mahoney, M. (1977). Publication prejudices: An experimental study of confirmatory bias in the peer review system. *Cognitive Therapy and Research*, 1: 161–75.

Research instruments

♦ Dianne Hinds

Introduction

Research is usually constructed through rigorous, systematic inquiry, and research instruments are the tools you use to collect and structure data thus transforming it into useful information. There are a number of possible approaches to carrying out your research. These include the survey, case study and experiment. The survey is concerned with gathering data from, usually, a large number of people (or respondents), and the data gathered usually focuses on the views, ideas and attitudes of those respondents in relation to the research topic. The case study draws on a specific environment, such as a school, and explores the research topic in relation to that school. This may involve obtaining the views of the teachers, children and parents and observing the day-to-day operation of the school. Experimental research is concerned with establishing the effect of some action upon two groups or situations. Typically, one of the two groups is known as a 'control' group, the other is known as the 'experiment' group. Control groups are used to examine whether changes might have taken place anyway (without the action), and experiment groups are used to explore the effect of the action. In all research strategies and approaches, but probably more so in experimental research, you should aim to develop procedures which produce results that are both *reliable* and *valid*.

Reliability

Refers to matters such as the consistency of a measure – for example, the likelihood of the same results being obtained if the procedures were repeated.

Validity

Relates broadly to the extent to which the measure achieves its aim, i.e. the extent to which an instrument measures what it claims to measure, or tests what it is intended to test.

All of these approaches to research draw upon a variety of instruments, and in this chapter we will look at a range of research instruments used to gather data for these different strategies.

Questionnaires

Questionnaires are useful tools for collecting data from a large number of respondents. Designing a good questionnaire can be a skilled and challenging technical activity. Therefore think very carefully before deciding to use one; in your case it may not necessarily be the most appropriate tool for data collection. The box below indicates where questionnaires might appropriately be used.

Use a questionnaire when:

♦ Information is sought from large numbers over a relatively large geographical area.
♦ The information sought is not complex.
♦ You are seeking information about facts, either in the present, or because of the influence of memory, in the recent past.
♦ You want to study particular groups, or people in a particular problem area because you want to generalise about them, make comparisons with other groups or use their responses and comparisons for development.
♦ You are certain that a questionnaire will produce the type of information you need.
♦ You are certain that barriers such as language and literacy do not apply to your population.

Developing questionnaires

Developing a questionnaire is a time-consuming process, therefore planning is crucial. The preparation of the questionnaire will include the 'total package' – including the covering letter in the case of a postal questionnaire. Create a time-line and plan for delays (see Chapter 2 for more detail about this). Clarity and a clear plan of action are essential elements of the design process. Also, remind yourself of what information you need. In addition to the actual construction of the questionnaire, you will need to make arrangements for piloting, distribution, and return. You will probably have only one opportunity in distributing the instrument to 'get it right', therefore piloting and amendments need to be carried out at an early stage. It is also useful to bear in mind the following key questions in the questionnaire design stage.

Key questions when designing questionnaires

♦ To whom is the questionnaire directed?
♦ Are you sure the instrument will be received and acted on by that person?
♦ How will you structure your questions?
♦ How will you process the returns?
♦ How will you analyse the responses?
♦ How can you design your questionnaire to enhance your response rate?

You might aim to consider this as a collaborative venture, in that the respondent is going to cooperate voluntarily. Your questionnaire should be user-friendly to obtain maximum cooperation, and the courtesies of 'please' and 'thank you' should not be underestimated. Outline the aims and purposes of the study and provide a contact number for those seeking further information. In some instances it might be useful to offer a copy of the completed report to interested participants as a way of thanking them for their time and effort in completing the questionnaire.

Ethics

The 1998 Data Protection Act requires that respondents should be informed if computerised data entry is part of your study. Respondents also have certain rights over their personal data, such as access to it. From 2001 similar safeguards will be required for manual records as for computer records. If you are using a questionnaire it might be helpful to print on the document that you may be using a computer to analyse the data.

You need to consider how responses will be analysed, so it is important at the planning and design stage to make decisions about any statistical analysis of your data. For example, will you add or tally the number of Yes/No responses to a particular question? Will you split male and female responses? Are you interested in the similarity of different types of respondents' answers to the same question? It is often too late to consider this when your data is returned. Initially some form of coding will be necessary to aid your eventual analysis of the data generated. In terms of questionnaire layout, coding boxes should be located on the right-hand side of the page to be read quickly and enable computerised data entry to take place.

Open and closed questions

The questions in your questionnaire will either be open or closed questions. Open questions allow the respondent to insert his or her views, ideas or suggestions about the question posed (Figure 4.1) Closed questions require that the respondent chooses one or more from a pre-defined category of 'answers' to the question. There are advantages and disadvantages to both open and closed questions in terms of analysing answers or responses. Responses to closed questions can be *pre-coded* (see Figure 4.2) which can be done in advance of circulating the

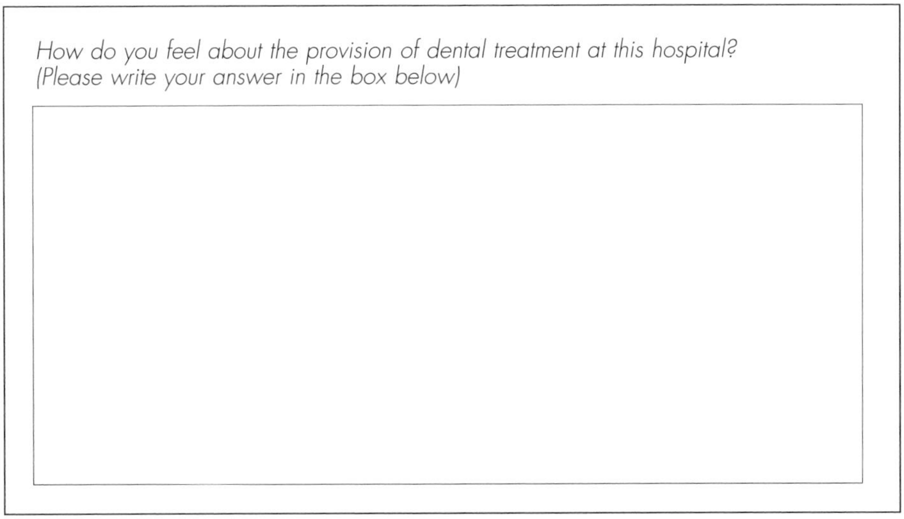

How do you feel about the provision of dental treatment at this hospital?
(Please write your answer in the box below)

FIGURE 4.1 Example of an open question

Question
Pre-coding
Gender:
Please tick the box below that most accurately describes you.
Male □ 1
Female □ 0
Marital status:
Please tick the box that most accurately describes you.
Married □ 1
Single □ 0

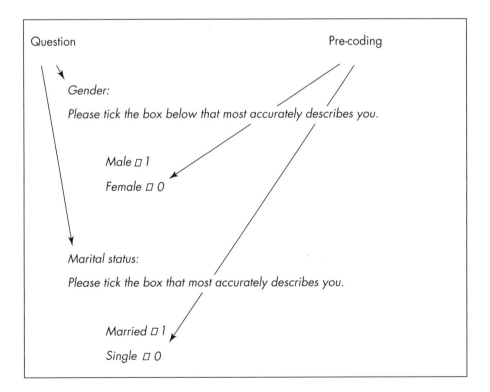

FIGURE 4.2 Examples of closed questions

questionnaire. This will help to speed up the analysis. However, the categories are the researcher's and may or may not reflect those of the respondent. Respondents are instructed to select from the available options, which may be limited to two, as when a Yes/No answer is offered. However, a more sophisticated series of alternatives may also be developed. Responses to open questions can only be coded after receipt by the researcher. This *post-coding* task adds more time to the analysis stage but the responses you analyse are the respondents' own.

Piloting is particularly important to ensure respondents don't misunderstand the questions you have asked. Additionally, it is critical to avoid leading questions worded to suggest that there is only one answer. Your vocabulary should also be clear, concise and avoid technical or redundant language. Every question should work for you and your respondents, therefore pre-testing will help reveal any problematic areas.

Points to remember when designing a questionnaire

♦ Aim for a maximum question sentence length of 20 words.
♦ There should be no hidden assumptions in your questions.
♦ Avoid double-barrelled questions.
♦ Avoid questions using negatives.
♦ Be sensitive to potentially irritating questions.
♦ Questionnaires should not be any longer or shorter than they need to be.

Detail paid to a range of design and layout aspects can enhance response rates. The presentation of the document should appeal to the respondent allowing him or her plenty of space for responses.

Effective distribution

At the planning stage decisions should be made about how to distribute your questionnaire and what to do about non-responses. Serial numbers may be allocated to individual documents to easily identify them.

Sometimes internal systems within an organisation may be used for question-naire distribution. In schools 'satchel post' may be used as a communication channel with parents. Similarly, being able to hand out questionnaires in person, particularly to a captive audience after a meeting or other event, may maximise your response rate. Personal contact often encourages cooperation.

Part of the design package for the distribution of a postal questionnaire should include a covering letter, together with a stamped addressed envelope. The letter should politely request the return of the questionnaire by an identified day and date.

Getting a good response

Maintain a detailed record of questionnaire distribution and return dates. An initial good response is likely to be followed by a gradual decline. If a decision has been made to follow up non-respondents, a second letter and questionnaire may be sent. The second letter should reiterate the significance of the study and state how much the personal contribution of the respondent is valued, or alternatively a telephone contact with the person responsible for questionnaire completion may encourage cooperation. Cohen and Manion (1980) cite a response rate of 40 per cent in a well-conducted postal survey, indicating that with appropriate reminders this may be increased to 70 or 80 per cent. Incentives can effectively be used to enhance response rates. These often consist of entering the respondent's name in a free prize draw.

Before coding, a process of questionnaire-checking or editing has to take place. In the case of self-completion questionnaires this tidying process aims to identify errors and omissions made by respondents.

One-to-one interviews

Interviews can vary in their structure. They can be focused on a given set of pre-defined questions that are covered in turn (known as a structured interview), or they can focus on a pre-defined theme or area and allow a discussion to take place between researcher and interviewee on that theme (known as an unstructured interview). In many interview situations a mixture of the two approaches is used, where some structured questions are asked followed by the exploration of general themes related to those questions.

Use interviews when

- ♦ In-depth information is required.
- ♦ Where the subject matter is potentially sensitive.
- ♦ The issues under examination would benefit from development or clarification.

It is important when planning your interview to consider the information the interviewee might reasonably need to know, the location of the interview, the recording of the interview, its subsequent write-up or transcription and analysis.

Prior to the interview you will probably have informed your interviewee on the area of research, either by telephone or by letter, and given a guideline on the anticipated length of interview. If the interview is to be tape-recorded, then consent should be sought. The respondent should be advised of the potential audience of the research, and given assurances about anonymity and confidentiality. Any arrangements for 'member checking', or transcript return should be offered to the interviewee. The setting should be carefully chosen, with minimum outside or distracting noise. Also, try to ensure that no interruptions are likely to take place and that chairs are carefully placed in the room at a comfortable distance apart. If a tape recorder is being used, the tape should be inserted (and checked). It is often helpful at the planning stage to pilot your interview with a friend or colleague who could provide constructive feedback on your interviewing performance.

Conducting the interview

Your interviewee should be made to feel comfortable, so begin the interview by thanking them for cooperating and assisting with your work. This helps to establish a relaxed attitude.

Any encounter between two people involves conscious and unconscious elements. Besides the verbal aspects of the interaction, non-verbal communication also affects the encounter both in obvious and more subtle ways. Both body language and eye contact are important and you may wish to record or note an interviewee's body language or eye contact when you cover a particularly important question or theme. For example, they may adopt an aggressive pose when answering questions covering subjects they feel strongly about. It may also be useful to mirror the interviewee's body language occasionally to encourage rapport.

If tape-recording an interview it is helpful to advise informants that your eyes may occasionally follow the progress of the tape – thus removing any possibility of anxiety regarding a perceived lack of attention. If possible, use a 60-minute interview tape with a separate conference or lapel microphone. Try not to use a pocket tape recorder with a built-in microphone, as many internal microphones seem to interfere with the quality of the taped material.

Without use of a tape or video recorder some method of creating an account of the event is necessary. Taking notes is one possibility, but this may be difficult to maintain whilst giving full attention to the content of the interview. If you do take notes attempt only to note key points made by the interviewee rather than trying to record everything they say. Your notes should act as a reminder of what was said at the time.

However you record and note your interview, you should be aware of problems of bias. It is important to recognise that when conducting an interview you should record the responses made by interviewees as accurately as possible. Your own preferences or, perhaps, stake in the outcome of the interview should remain secondary. You should record accurately what was said and not what you think should have been said. Robson (1993) notes that many of these 'biases', such as selective attention, are familiar to psychologists and they can be present in both the interviewer's and interviewee's mind.

As the interview draws to a conclusion I frequently ask the informant whether they have anything to add to the interview that has not been addressed by any of my questions or their responses. This helps avoid a situation where the respondent is prompted to add to the interview following the conclusion of the interview. All interviews should conclude with a heartfelt message of thanks from the interviewer. Some very privileged researchers are fortunate to find themselves thanked for a process that participants have experienced as therapeutic, or developmental in some way.

Transcription and analysis

Tapes require transcription and analysis. Transcription takes time, to the extent that advice on my first research project included allowing a ratio of 10:1 between collecting data and the resultant transcription and analysis of that data. For every hour spent interviewing allow ten times as much time to process the data. Writing up your notes into a full account as soon as practically possible following data collection has the advantage of capturing all, or most, of what was said, as it will still be fresh in your mind.

Focus group interviews

There can be few individuals who have not heard of focus groups. Political parties use them, opposition parties spurn their efforts and television companies are reported to amend their programmes following analysis of focus group responses. The process is based on the principles of self-disclosure, grounded in a comfortable environment, a particular type of questioning, and the establishment of focus group rules. Generally numbering between seven to ten individuals, groups have been conducted with a minimum of four. Beyond twelve participants the group tends to fragment. The mix will probably consist of strangers, or people slightly acquainted with one another, but there will be similarities between them.

Kreuger (1994) recommends that two people conduct the focus group. One (the moderator) may attend to the questions, and the second can record the interactions, noting nodding and other non-verbal behaviour, which may indicate the extent of agreement, for instance. Compared with one-to-one interviews, the questioner in a focus group interview situation plays the role of a 'facilitator', rather than a 'director' of the proceedings. Once the general topic for discussion has been fixed to everyone's satisfaction, he or she is responsible for shaping and steering the path the participants themselves have chosen to tread. In contrast to one-to-one interviews, the job of determining the precise content of the discussion within the boundaries of the topic as a whole is deliberately left to the participants. The reasoning behind this lies in the implication that those aspects of the topic most important, meaningful or relevant to the participants will emerge first in the interview. It is important that the interviewer encourages comments of all types, both positive and negative, taking care to avoid making judgements about responses and controlling body language communicating approval or disapproval (Kreuger 1994).

When to use a focus group inquiry

- ◆   To gain information relating to how people think.
- ◆   To explain perceptions of an event, idea or experience.
- ◆   When there is a desire for more understanding of the human experience.
- ◆   When seeking the perspective of the client.

Ethnography

With some research approaches, you may be required to observe directly the activities of members of a particular social group with a view to providing an accurate description or evaluation of those activities. This is ethnography. Essentially, there are two forms of ethnography – participant and non-participant observations. With participant observation you as researcher are a part of the situation you are observing. For example, you could be involved with a meeting you are recording for your research, or you may be exploring the way your work environment changes due to the introduction of new working practices. Non-participant observation involves you as researcher being more detached from the meeting you are observing. For example, you may be present at the meeting but, as a non-participant, you will have no input or effect on the meeting.

Advantages and disadvantages of ethnography

Advantages
- ◆ Direct evidence of the event or process under study.
- ◆ The active role of researcher as research instrument requires little technical support.
- ◆ Data produced may offer insights into the complex realities of the setting.

Disadvantages
- ◆ To be both participant and observer in a sustained process requires particular qualities when studying the lives and activities of others.
- ◆ Opportunities to access settings may be limited.

It is important when planning your observations to consider carefully the kind of information you want to collect. Is the focus of the inquiry to be on the content or process of an event or meeting, for example, or how the members of the meeting interact? Also, are the observations to be based on the actions and activities of individuals or groups?

When recording your observations note the context of the event. A general description of the time, place, setting and participants is a valuable adjunct to any data collection. Sensitivity to the atmosphere and noting any key events, which may include the late arrival of a particular person, helps contextualise activities. Charts and seating plans will help to identify participants in a group setting, but beyond the physical environment an observation schedule, whether self-designed or commercially available, will require a specific recording method. To assist the observation process, observation schedules, such as Flanders Interaction Analysis (Flanders 1970), are often used. The Flanders Interaction Analysis model is an example of a systematic observation framework for analysing, for example, teacher and pupil behaviour in the classroom. Ten or so categories describe behaviour and these guide the observer's coding of the interactions that take place. Categories may include 'shows tension release' (jokes, laughs, shows satisfaction) and 'shows antagonism' (deflates others' status, defends or asserts self).

Diaries

The diary is a useful method of gathering routine information relating to particular activities. This method involves participants being requested to keep an account of the behaviour or activity under study within an identified time frame. Recently, this approach has been used in the health services through the use of the patient diary as a research tool. This can provide a useful insight into, for instance, the patient experience following surgery (although in the hospital setting this probably requires the approval of the Ethics Committee).

Uses of the diary

◆ Used as a form of self-completed observation schedule.
◆ As a model of self-completed questionnaire.
◆ Combined with other instruments – for example using a diary prior to interview, specifically to generate questions.

The frequency of use of the diary will depend upon your research questions. If you have a clear set of questions, a more structured form of diary may be appropriate – this could include sections dedicated to specific tasks performed through the day. Decisions about data analysis will depend on the prior structure of the instrument. Pre-defined categories will provide a basic structure for analysis, whilst a more unstructured instrument may itself be used as a model for category development.

It is important when using the diary as a research instrument to provide explicit instructions in order to ensure the diary is completed in a manner fitting the aims of the research questions. For this reason careful piloting is necessary, and the diary should be planned with the same care and preparation as a questionnaire. Potentially, diary accounts offer a wealth of information and, as technology advances, electronic diaries would appear to offer enormous potential as a method of data collection readily structured for subsequent analysis.

Disadvantages of using diaries

◆ This method places a considerable responsibility on the respondent, and there may be some problems with self-recording.
◆ The time required for diary completion may prove too demanding.
◆ The representativeness of the activities recorded may be problematic and introduce bias.

Content analysis

'Content analysis is a technique that enables researchers to study human behaviour in an indirect way' (Fraenkel and Wallen 2000: 469). This useful research tool involves the examination or analysis of the contents of a communication. This could include analysing newspaper articles, journal contents, magazines, speeches, advertisements and so on. Analysing communications allows us, for example, to explore the writer's own ideas, beliefs and attitudes relating to the subject matter. To begin the analysis we must build up categories or ratings or scores that can be applied across the range of material being analysed. The coding of data is discussed further in Chapter 6.

Essentially three types of content analysis can take place: an analysis of the number of times a specific word or phrase is used (for example, how many times televisions are mentioned in material discussing leisure time); an analysis across a range of material to establish if a topic or theme is or is not raised (for example, whether articles covering library use mention opening hours); and an analysis that seeks more than one topic or category (for example, how many times televisions are mentioned by males as opposed to females).

The 'steps in content analysis' box shows the key points to bear in mind when contemplating a content analysis.

Steps in content analysis

1   Conduct an initial 'exploratory data analysis' for questions emerging from the data.
2   Decide your recording unit – this may be the individual word, sentences, paragraphs, themes or characters. In some instances the examination of the context may be necessary (such as the remainder of the sentence).
3   Construct categories for analysis. It is necessary to have a clear view of the potential categories or issues that might be presented in the text.
4   Code the units to reflect the categories. The text needs careful scrutiny to code all relevant units, whether words or sentences. The codes may be written on the text, or entered via a computer.
5   As codes are defined write a careful description of the category. This might be useful in refreshing your own memory at a later stage in the research.
6   The frequency of the unit should be counted – analysis may include a tally of the times units occur.

Using computers with research instruments

Highly sophisticated computer programs now exist to aid the design, collation and analysis of research instruments and the data they help to collect. Many operate at a variety of levels depending upon the assistance you require. Some offer assistance in questionnaire design, covering layout and pre-coding issues, others assist with the analysis and testing of your data. Lexica is a program that adds to textual analysis and claims to perform complex lexical analysis. Beyond these applications modules are available which assist the creation of multimedia and Internet surveys.

Qualitative data analysis programs such as Nudist and Ethnograph are perhaps the most widely used programs for the analysis of qualitative data. Further information relating to qualitative data analysis packages can be found in *Qualitative Research: Analysis Types and Software* (Tesch 1990) and *Computer Analysis and Qualitative Research* (Fielding and Lee 1998).

References and further reading

Cohen, L. and Manion L. (1980) *Research Methods in Education*. Beckenham: Croom Helm.

Fielding, N. G. and Lee. R. M. (1998) *Computer Analysis and Qualitative Research*. London: Sage.

Flanders, N. A. (1970) *Analysing Teacher Behaviour*. Cambridge, MA: Addison-Wesley.

Fraenkel, J. R. and Wallen, N. E. (2000) *How to Design and Evaluate Research in Education* (fourth edition). New York: McGraw Hill.

Krueger, R. (1994) *Focus Groups. A Practical Guide for Applied Research*. London: Sage.

Robson, C. (1993) *Real World Research*. Oxford: Blackwell.

Tesch, R. (1990) *Qualitative Research: Analysis Types and Software Tools*. London: Falmer Press.

Finding and locating information

♦ Lesley Gray

Introduction

One of the key skills for any research student or researcher is being able to retrieve and locate information. Information and information resources need to be searched for and retrieved when required and must be both relevant and up-to-date.

There are a vast number of information resources available in a wide variety of formats, such as printed volumes, CD-ROMs or on-line services delivered via the Web. Advances in electronic and telecommunications technology have resulted in a proliferation of material from both traditional or formal publishers and private or self-published material. Not only does the researcher need to be aware of the diversity and amount of information that is available, but also of issues relating to the quality and reliability of the information, and the difficulties associated with locating all available information – much of which may be produced unsystematically.

There is such a wide range of information resources available to researchers, that it is impossible to provide a totally comprehensive survey of all information sources. Due to the nature of the discipline, there is much overlap between various aspects of education and other aspects of the social sciences, such as sociology, as well as psychology.

One of the difficulties in writing a chapter such as this is that much of the information and references to information resources and web sites is out of date before it even reaches publication. New information sources are being published all the time, and the nature of information provision is changing rapidly as well. Developments in computer and communications technology have made an enormous impact on information provision over the last ten years – and signs

---

5 steps to be followed in any search for information

Orientate: Orientate yourself with the resources available to you, starting with the library that you will be using, the range of resources that are available to you, and with the resource that you will be searching. This may include learning to use the technology required to consult the resource such as a CD-ROM or the World Wide Web.

Search: Plan your search, select your search tools, decide on your search strategy, select search terms and then perform the search.

Locate: Select items retrieved by the search and then identify how and where to locate the selected resources. Items may be located within your local library or perhaps in another library, or they may be available from a database held locally or accessible across a network.

Evaluate: Once the information resource has been located, then both the content and the resource should be evaluated for reliability, currency, relevance and authorship.

Record: A record, which may take the form of notes, needs to be made of the resource and its contents or any relevant information which you can consult when required.

---

indicate that the rate of development is not likely to decrease in the near future. The development and exploitation of the World Wide Web has had a great impact on access to information, and it has become both an important source of information and a universal interface for access to information. The dynamic nature of the Web means that web sites, databases, and information sources are changing continuously and what may be available at one site today, may not be there a day later.

Where to start

Your supervisor

Your supervisor or manager may be familiar with the key literature on the subject and may be able to give you, or refer you to, key references or the names of researchers in the field, which could provide you with a good starting point.

The library

The library in your department or university is an obvious point to begin a search for information. The librarian will be able to advise you on the library facilities, the range of resources and services that are available to you as a researcher – both within the institution and with other local libraries – and related organisations. Library services may include on-line services that the library or organisation subscribes to, as well as facilities such as inter-library loans, photocopying and printing facilities. Library staff will also be able to inform you of copyright issues, and could advise you on reciprocal borrowing rights with other libraries available to you in the area.

To use a library effectively, you need to become be familiar with its physical environment and layout, the way in which its resources are organised and learn how to use the search tools – such as catalogues and bibliographic databases – to locate information resources. If you are unfamiliar with on-line searching or the use of any resources, the library staff will be able to assist you. Some libraries organise on request, or offer regular sessions to train library users in the use of electronic resources. If you are unfamiliar with the use of any resources, ask library staff for assistance when required. It may be possible, and often preferable, to book a session for a time that is suitable to library staff and you.

Many librarians are subject and information specialists. As subject specialists, librarians have a thorough knowledge of a subject or discipline, especially with regard to the range of subject-related information sources that are available both within the organisation and beyond. They will be familiar with the material in the library's own collection, and how and where to locate items in the library. Librarians are information specialists trained in organisation and retrieval of information and information resources. They are familiar with literature-searching and with the use of a range of search tools. They will be able to show you how to use the catalogue and indexes to locate items held in the collection and may also be able to advise you of relevant sources to search, as well as search strategies and search terms to use.

Many libraries offer current awareness services for academic and research staff, and research students. The current awareness service may be informal, with the library informing you when new material on your topic of interest is processed and available for loan, or formal. A research or interest profile may be compiled during a meeting or by the completion of a form, and kept on file in the library. When new material or new issues of journals are received by the library, the contents pages and subject coverage of the items are scanned and matched against the profiles, and readers notified of new items of potential interest available in the library.

Locating information and information resources

Search tools

♦ Library catalogues
♦ Indexes and abstracting journals or services
♦ Internet search engines

Library catalogues

A library catalogue systematically lists a collection of records that contain bibliographic information about items held in the library collection. Each catalogue record describes an item, identifying it uniquely with author, title and other bibliographic details, as well as the location of the item within the library. A library catalogue provides information about the 'physical' items in the collection, but does not provide access to the contents of the item. Articles in periodicals or chapters in books are not usually indexed in a library catalogue.

This is the key local bibliographic resource that provides listings and details of items held in the library in your institution or organisation. The records in the library catalogue may cover a wide range of materials such as books, reports, theses, pamphlets, videos and ephemera. Library catalogues were traditionally print or card catalogues, but most libraries have computer catalogues now. These are referred to as OPACs (On-Line-Public-Access-Catalogues).

Other library catalogues

National library catalogues
British Library on-line catalogue, OPAC97 http://opac97.bl.uk/
OPAC97 contains records for material that is held in the British Library in the major reference collections (London) and the Document Supply collections of the British Library held at the Document Supply Centre (BLDSC) at Boston Spa.

Library of Congress (USA) Online Catalog http://catalog.loc.gov/
This is a database of approximately 12 million records representing books, serials, computer files, manuscripts, cartographic materials, music, sound recordings, and visual materials held in the in the Library's collections.

National Library Catalogues Worldwide http://www.library.uq.edu.au/ssah/jeast/

University and research libraries

COPAC http://www.copac.ac.uk/
COPAC (Consortium of University and Research Libraries On-line Public Access Catalogue) gives access to the on-line catalogues of some of the largest university research libraries in the UK and Ireland. A link is provided to the Web pages of each of the contributing libraries.

It is possible to access other library catalogues via the Internet. Searching these catalogues will provide you with references to sources that are not held in your local library so you will not have immediate access to the items or the information that they contain. It may be possible to visit the library that holds the item, to request the item on inter-library loan or to ask your library if they would consider purchasing the item.

National libraries are responsible for collecting all publications issued in their respective countries. A national library catalogue is a comprehensive source of publications issued in a country, and as such, can be a useful resource when searching for information. The on-line catalogues of a national library may not list all the older material held in the library's collections as not all national libraries have automated all records yet.

The catalogues of other university libraries, as well as many research libraries are available on the Internet via HYTELNET, or the NISS Higher Education gateway (http://www.niss.ac.uk/). The COPAC (Consortium of University and Research Libraries Online Public Access Catalogue) database provides access to the records of items held in some of the largest university research libraries in the UK and Ireland.

Indexes

Indexing and abstracting journals or services (as the electronic forms are known) are essential tools for research staff and students. They provide access to the information or contents of various types of publication: articles in journals, newspapers, chapters in books, reports, theses, as well as a range of other types of publication. Indexes and abstracting journals are available in several formats: in print and micro-format, and database format on CD-ROM or on-line, or both.

In general, indexes and abstracting services provide access to each article which is indexed by author and title, and generally also has a subject entry. Abstracting journals also provide the abstract from the article itself, and some foreign articles may include an English abstract. This distinction is not as clear-cut as it was before, as many indexes that are available in electronic format now include abstracts as well (for example, ERIC). Indexes may be multidisciplinary, covering a broad subject area, such as the social sciences, subject specific, or index records from a particular form of publication such as newspapers or theses.

A citation index contains lists of published documents that reference or 'cite' a given work by a given author. Each article in the database includes a list of the references that are cited in the article, and the index brings together all indexed articles that cite a particular reference. It is possible to search for a particular author or search term, and find other articles that have cited the same work and may be of relevance. In cases where other resources retrieve few relevant references, citation searching may uncover other authors writing on the same or related subjects that can be followed up, or indicate a change in terminology or thinking and lead to other sources of information that had perhaps not been considered before. It is possible to trace how articles or books have been commented on, and how theories and works have developed chronologically. Significant or important works are likely to have been widely cited. It is important to be aware that retrieved citations may contain errors, as the originator's list of citations are not checked for spelling errors of author names and variations in the initials used and the cited work (usually a journal title) may be heavily and sometimes inconsistently abbreviated.

Indexes and abstracting services

Education indexes
British Educational Index (BEI)
This is an important resource for educational research in Great Britain. This index includes references to 350 British and selected European English language periodicals (and an increasing amount of national report and conference literature) in the field of education and training. The print version indexes periodical literature from 1954 while coverage of the electronic versions extends back to 1975. The *Australian Education Index* and *the Canadian Education Index* are also available in the same format, and together with BEI are available as a dataset called *International ERIC*.

British education index. University of Leeds, 1954– .
International ERIC. [CD-ROM]. Updated quarterly. Dialog, 1975– .
British education index. [On-line]. Updated monthly. [Part of BIDS Education Service], 1986 – .

ERIC
ERIC (Educational Resources Information Center) database is sponsored by the US Department of Education. It indexes over 775 periodicals and contains more than 700,000 records and has an international coverage. Entries in the database generally include an abstract of the article or item. Research documents, journal articles, reports, technical reports, program descriptions and evaluations, and curricular materials are indexed. The electronic version of ERIC consists of 2 indexes which are available in print

(continued)

form as *Research in Education* (RIE) and *Current Index to Journals in Education* (CIJE).

Other indexes

Periodicals contents index. [Online & CD-ROM]. Chadwyck Healey
PCI contains information from the tables of contents of thousands of English and other European language journals, from their first year of publication up to 1990. It is an important resource for historical research as it provides access to older periodical literature not available from other indexing and abstracting services.

British Newspaper Index. [Electronic]. Quarterly. Primary Source media. 1992–
This database indexes the following newspapers: *Times, Sunday Times, Times Education Supplement, Times Higher Education Supplement, Times Literary Supplement, Daily Telegraph. Sunday Telegraph, Independent, Independent on Sunday* and the *Observer*.

Psychological Abstracts. 12 pa. American Psychological Association, 1955– .
PsycLIT. [CD-ROM]. Quarterly. American Psychological Association. Silver Platter Information, 1974– .

Social Sciences Citation Index. **[Online]. Weekly. Institute of Scientific Information (ISI) 1981–**
SOCIAL SCISEARCH, a component of ISI, corresponds to the print index Social Sciences Citation Index, a multidisciplinary index to the journal literature of the behavioural and social sciences. More than 1,400 periodical titles are covered, with selected relevant items from a further 3,100 physical and natural science titles. The index includes articles, editorials, letters and reviews, and abstracts are available for many of the records. Non-journal literature, such as conference literature or books, is not included. SOCIAL SCISEARCH features citation indexing, enabling you to search for papers which have referenced a known paper or other work.

Internet

A vast amount of information is available via the Internet. Retrieval of information is widely recognised as a significant problem and searching for and locating information can be time-consuming and confusing.

Searching is a process fundamental to using the Internet effectively, but one that is difficult, as the number of web sites and the pages that they host increases daily. Sites may disappear or move to new locations as quickly as they appeared, making it difficult for users to access the information again. The number of search services available for searching the web also increases and diversifies. It is important that you realise that various search engines differ in coverage, search facilities and processes, and in the results that are retrieved and displayed. It is important to be aware of the strengths and weaknesses of the different search engines.

WEB DIRECTORIES AND SEARCH ENGINES

Web directories are created and maintained by humans. Editors index web sites that have been submitted to the service, which are selected according to various qualitative and content criteria. Because these services are labour intensive and selective in the sites that are indexed, only a tiny percentage of available information is covered, although the sites retrieved have been selected by humans for inclusion in the directory. When using web directories, it is important to try more than one directory when searching for information, as there can be major differences in their listings.

Web search engines search a database of indexed web sites. When you enter your search terms, the script interrogates the database, and the results are presented in a dynamically generated web page. The search engine database is built up by programs (called spiders or crawlers) that constantly search the Web for new pages, index words on those pages, and then match the indexed word with the URL site of the page on which it appears. Because they run automatically and index so many web pages, search engines may often find information not listed in directories, although they actually cover only a small percentage of information available on the Web.

Search engines will only index web pages that have been created specifically for the Web. Many web sites produce dynamically created pages containing information extracted on request by the searcher from a database – information that does not exist in web page format until the query is received – and so will not be found by a search engine.

Metasearch sites enable the user to search across several search engines and web directories simultaneously. They allow you to search several services simultaneously and view the results in one list. These search facilities are slow and may retrieve only a small number of the total number of hits.

Searching the Internet

Web directories	Yahoo	http://www.yahoo.com
	UK Index	http://www.ukindex.co.uk/
Web search	Altavista	http://www.altavista.com/
engines	Infoseek(now	
	called GO)	http://infoseek.go.com/
	Lycos	http://www.lycos.com/
Metasearch sites	SavvySearch	http://www.savvysearch.com/
	Meta Crawler	http://www.metacrawler.com/index.html

INFORMATION ON THE WEB

It is necessary to evaluate the content and source of any information resource that you retrieve. When using information on the Internet, this is of particular importance as information may be posted by anyone and is not subject to any form of quality control, authenticity checks or scrutiny by a publisher. When viewing any site, it is worthwhile to check the following: the source, originator or owner of the material, the date of the information source, the frequency of updating and the date of the last update.

There are, however, a number of sites that provide links to selected, authoritative information sites. Many libraries provide a web interface to their library and information services, often including access to the library catalogue, electronic resources, as well as links to other sites of interest. Gateway services are particularly useful sites as they list and provide links to information sources that have been selected and evaluated by subject or information specialists. There are several subject gateways for the social sciences and education. NISS (National Information Services and Systems) gathers together and provides links to selected information services for the UK academic community and has links to a wide range of education sites. Social Science Information Gateway (SOSIG) site is an 'on-line catalogue' of Internet resources for the social sciences, which have been selected, evaluated and classified by subject specialists. These include reports, papers, electronic journals, newsletters and discussion lists and also has a subject listings to help to locate resources for a particular subject area (see http://www.sosig. ac.uk/).

The Internet is a good source of information of documents published by, and information provided by, governmental and other public and private agencies such at the Department for Education and Employment (DFEE), the School Curriuclum

Assessment Authority (SCAA), now the Qualifications and Curriulum Authority (QCA), the National Foundation for Educational Research (NFER) and the Office for Standards in Education (OFSTED).

Education on the Internet

Subject gateways

NISS (National Information Services and Systems)	http://www.niss.ca.uk/
SOSIG (Social Sciences Information Gateway)	http://www.sosig.ac.uk/
Education-line	http://www.leeds.ac.uk/educol/

Official education sites

DFEE (Department for Education and Employment)	http://www.dfee.gov.uk/
OFSTED (Office for Standards in Education)	http://www.ofsted.gov.uk/
QCA (Qualifications and Curriculum Authority)	http://www.qca.org.uk/menu.htm
TTA (Teacher Training Agency)	http://www.teach-tta.gov.uk
Government statistical service	http://www.statistics.gov.uk/
Office for National Statistics	http://www.ons.gov.uk/

European sites

euroguide	http://www.euroguide.org/about.htm
EURYDICE	http://www.eurydice.org/
European Commission: Education & Culture	http://europa.eu.int/comm/education/info.html

---

Selecting the resource to search: manual vs. on-line searching

Many information sources are now available in a variety of formats: print and electronic (CD-ROMs and on-line databases). In the first instance, your choice of format of an information resource will depend on the availability of that resource to you. Many of the resources mentioned in this chapter are available in print and electronic format, although the titles may differ slightly from format to format.

Many of the on-line services are closed services and require institutional subscriptions, and access is password controlled. The librarian will be able to advise if the on-line facilities are available to you, and to which services the organisation subscribes. Due to the costs of subscriptions to print and electronic information sources, you may not have access to an unlimited range of resources. Online searching introduces a flexibility of search not possible in print-based systems. Computers can manipulate large amounts of data quickly, and can provide access to information via a large number of access points. Some on-line and CD-ROM databases also provide or facilitate access to the full text of electronic journals through links, or may contain the full text of articles or texts. Manual searches, using print-based systems, can be slow and time-consuming – as a result many items may be missed or overlooked. Electronic resources usually contain a substantial resource of references covering a large number of journal titles. Bibliographic details of retrieved references can be saved to file or printed, and are generally accurate and complete.

Indexes and abstracts available in electronic format on CD-ROM or on-line are easier and faster to use that their print counterparts. However, they do require that the user become familiar with the technology involved, and with using a range of search interfaces and search facilities in order to retrieve the relevant information from the system. Online information services available via the Internet are more frequently updated, and information becomes accessible as soon as it becomes available. CD-ROM and print versions are updated on a regular basis, although there may be a delay of several months between updates.

Electronic databases may only provide access to a limited number of years of information. Although this differs from database to database, many databases will only contain 10 to 15 years of data. Digitisation or the re-entering of data is expensive, and so print resources will need to be consulted if older information sources are sought.

The inter-library loan facility

It is possible to make use of the inter-library loan facilities in order to obtain material that is necessary to your work but not locally available. No library can afford to purchase more than a proportion of the publications available on a particular subject today.

Requests for inter-library loans of journal articles are usually supplied in the form of a photocopy, while, when requesting books or theses, the item itself (or a microfilm) may be loaned to the library. There may also be a time delay in actually receiving the item. The library staff will be able to advise you on the procedures to be followed. In some organisations, the full cost or part of the cost is passed on to the requestor (either you or the project on which you are working), but this varies from place to place. It is therefore necessary when you are considering requesting an inter-library loan to be selective and request items that will be of relevance to you. Full and accurate bibliographic details are essential when making a request.

It may be possible to visit other libraries to consult material that is held in their collections. The librarian in your library could advise you on cooperative arrangements with other libraries such as the SCONUL Vacation scheme. Most libraries will allow you to use their collections and facilities for reference purposes but will not extend borrowing rights to you. Before visiting another library, it is advisable to contact the library that you hope to visit and obtain information about opening hours and any administrative requirements for your entry. Some libraries require a letter of introduction from your organisation or supervisor, while others require a written request to be submitted in advance of your visit.

Other information resources

Information resources can be categorised in many different ways: by the format of the resource (print or electronic), by content and subject, intended audience or reader or by the type of information that the resource contains, to name but a few. In this section, several types of information sources are discussed. A few examples of each type of source that may be useful to researchers are given, but serve only as possible resources or starting points in an information search. It is in no way intended to be a definitive list of resources.

JOURNALS OR PERIODICALS

Research or refereed journals contain reports of original research studies, which include detailed accounts of the methodology and results of the studies. They are valuable sources of current information, as the frequency of publication makes it possible to disseminate information more quickly than in books.

Many print journals are published simultaneously in electronic format. The on-line version may list the contents of the journal, selected articles or excepts of articles, or the full text of the journal. Some electronic titles are available on-line before the print edition. The full text of an electronic journal is searchable. Links in the text may provide access to other information sources, and multimedia technology allows some electronic journals to include colour graphics, sound and video clips in the articles.

Access to electronic journals is usually provided from links on the library web page. Several higher education initiatives and projects such as JSTOR, SuperJournal and CHEST (Combined Higher Education Software Team) are involved in negotiating with publishers and providing access to electronic journals for higher education institutions.

CONFERENCE PROCEEDINGS

Conference proceedings may be published in a variety of forms: as separately published volumes, as periodicals or supplements to periodicals, or distributed informally to conference participants. Conferences play an important role in the dissemination of information where new research and current issues are debated or made public. Conference proceedings may be of value to researchers in providing reviews of trends.

REFERENCE BOOKS

Reference sources generally cover a wide subject area, and are compiled to supply authoritative and definitive information. They may be of particular use for answering a quick enquiry or finding a fact quickly. Reference sources include dictionaries, encyclopaedias, source books, year books, indexes and bibliographies, which can also be used to get a brief overview of a topic. When starting a research project, the reference collection could be used to help you define the subject area of your study more closely. It may also be able to provide you with facts and figures as your research progresses.

RESEARCH REPORTS

Reports contain the results of, or progress made in, research projects, investigations and surveys. A report is usually issued by the funding or performing body and may not be commercially published. A wide range of organisations publish research reports. These include organisations such as the NFER, ESRC (Economic and Social Research Council), government and local authorities, university departments and other agencies. Many of these organisations make reports available via their web sites on the Internet. There are several publications that are available which list research in progress in the UK, such as the Register of Education Research in the UK, published by the NFER.

Theses and dissertations are submitted by the author for a higher degree or professional qualification or award. They report on an investigation or research project that has been carried out, and present the findings of the work and the conclusions reached. They are useful sources to consult as they are a source of information about work that has already been done in a particular field, and may be a source of references to other literature on a particular subject, as they generally incorporate a literature review. Theses and dissertations are unpublished works, so it is important to establish what the copyright regulations in each institution are when consulting and reporting on the information contained in them. The British Library collects most British theses submitted for doctoral degrees. Records for theses held by the British Library are located in the British Library on-line catalogue. Copies may be borrowed on microfilm or, in some cases, on microfiche via the inter-library loan system.

Newspapers are important sources of information of current events, and may have historical value. Many newspapers are now available on-line, although some services do require a subscription. On-line archives of previous editions is generally limited, although previous issues are available in a variety of formats including microfiche and CD-ROM. The *Times Educational Supplement* and *Times Higher Education Supplement* are useful sources for education researchers, although other broadsheets may have education supplements – for example, the *Guardian* which has a weekly education supplement.

Official publications refer to a wide range of publications produced by central government, government-funded departments, government-sponsored organisations or intergovernmental organisations such at the United Nations or the

European Community. This category of resources includes items issued by Parliament (Acts of Parliament, Command Papers, Select Committee Reports, Statutory Instruments) and non-Parliamentary organisations (HMI reports, DfEE, government agencies and ministries). Although an increasing number of these publications are available on-line on an organisation's web site on the Internet, many are available only in print format.

UKOP Online (http: //www.ukop.co.uk) is the complete catalogue of United Kingdom Official Publications from 1980 to the present day. It comprises detailed bibliographic and ordering information on the full range of official publications, whether published by The Stationery Office, or one of the other 500 bodies – ranging from Departments of State to quangos and ombudsmen, and British, European and international organisations – for whom the Stationery Office acts as agent.

STATISTICAL SOURCES

There are several major bodies whose purpose is to gather and coordinate statistics and official figures across the UK government, and to store this information in national archives. These include the Office for National Statistics, the Public Record Office, the General Register Office for Scotland, the Scottish Records Offices and the Northern Ireland Statistics and Research Agency. Many other major central government departments have their own research or statistics sections. These bodies make this information available via printed reports, and latterly, much of this information is available on the individual organisation's web site.

Example statistical information sources

- Government statistical service   http://www.statistics.gov.uk/
- Office for National Statistics   http://www.ons.gov.uk/
- Guide to official statistics. HMSO
- Office for National Statistics. 1970– . *Social trends: a publication of the Government Statistical Service.* No.1–. London: Stationery Office.

PEOPLE

Communicating with the people around you can also be a source of valuable information to a researcher. Information gathered in this way may result from formal conversations or communication with colleagues or specialists in the field of your research, and may take place at a conference or at meetings, or from informal discussions and communication between colleagues in the department, at the tea or lunch table, or via e-mail discussion groups. A wide range of e-mail discussion lists (http://www.mailbase.ac.uk) and bulletin boards are available, and provide an important forum for researchers and other interested people to share and exchange ideas.

A literature search strategy

A literature search is a systematic and thorough search of all types of published literature in order to identify as many items as possible that are relevant to a particular topic (Gash 1989). The search should include as wide a range of information sources as possible, including books, journal articles, reports, theses, government publications, and so on. A full literature search should not be confined only to material or items held in only one collection. The most effective search is one that is well thought out, properly planned and well recorded. The detail of conducting a traditional literature review is covered in Chapter 3. Below is guidance indicating the requirements of conducting a literature review using an electronic library catalogue or Internet-based catalogue.

Identify key concepts

You need to identify the key concepts or aspects of the information that you will need to search for in order to retrieve information relevant to your needs. From these key concepts, you will then select the search terms that you will use in your search.

Formulate your search strategy

Consider each of the key concepts that you have identified and develop related and alternative terms for each. The search terms that you select must be compatible with the terminology and bias of the resource to be searched. For example, when searching a database produced in America it is important to select terminology that would be in used in the USA and take into account differences in spelling or terms, for example, *elementary* instead of *primary* and *behavior* instead of *behaviour*. It may be helpful to identify related or alternative terms, broader and narrower terms and variations in spelling of terms as well.

Using your search statement, you need to identify the concepts or components as well as their relationships to one another. Boolean operators are used to construct a search strategy and allow you to specify how the resource will use the terms to search for the information you wish to retrieve: 'AND' will retrieve items that contain both search terms; 'OR' will retrieve items with either of the terms; while 'NOT' (which should be used with caution) will retrieve results that contain one of the search terms and NOT another (see Figure 5.1). Truncation or wildcards may also be used. Although the symbols may differ according to the search tool being used, the * and ? are widely used. Truncation, using the *, allows you to search for all variations of the stem of a term. For example, searching for *teach** will retrieve teach*er*, teach*ers*, teach*es*, teach*ing*, etc. Wildcards may be used to replace a single letter in a term, for example, *wom?n* will retrieve items with the terms wom*a*n and wom*e*n.

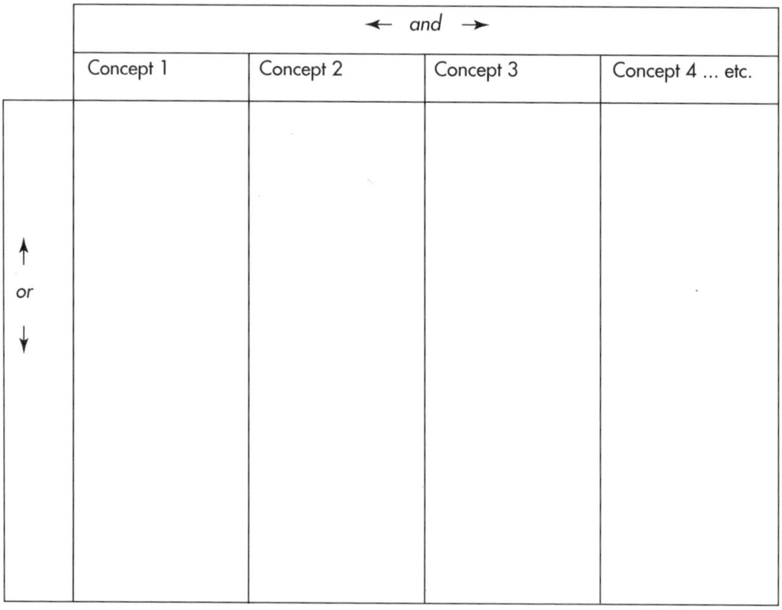

	← *and* →		
Concept 1	Concept 2	Concept 3	Concept 4 … etc.

or ↑↓

FIGURE 5.1 Example framework for a search

Select your resource

Selection of a resource to use for a literature search will depend on its suitability to the topic or area of interest that you wish to retrieve information on. A subject librarian will be able to advise you on available and suitable resources, as well as offering help with using the search tool and conducting the search.

Familiarise yourself with the resource that you are going to search. Each database has its own interface as well as its own rules for searching. It is necessary to find out how to enter search terms, specify which field is to be searched, and to perform a search. You will also need to know how to combine search terms and limit searches, as well as how to mark, save or print relevant references retrieved by the search. This also applies to print-based resources that you may be searching. It is important to make use of all sources of help available to you. Library staff will be able to assist you in the use of resources in the library, and most on-line and electronic resources have on-line help facilities to assist you.

Review search results

In order to determine whether the search terms have retrieved relevant information resources, you need to review the items that have been retrieved. It may be necessary to change the terms that you selected, to add additional terms or to remove terms that are retrieving irrelevant items. If your search retrieves too few or too many results, it may be necessary to broaden or limit your search. To broaden a search, you may consider using a broader term or removing a term. There are several ways to limit a search, including adding additional terms, imposing limits such as date, type or language of publication on the search, changing an OR operator to an AND operator between concepts.

Recording the search

It is a good idea to keep a record of the searches that you have done, as well as the name of the resource that you have searched. Keeping a record of each search that you do may save you time and effort in the long run. Repeating the search at regular intervals will retrieve new articles or items that have been published since your last search and will enable you to keep up-to-date with the latest research and developments in your field of interest. In the light of reading that you are doing, and results of your research, you may wish to repeat or broaden an earlier search to include new concepts or terminology. Searches may be recorded by keeping a note of search terms, and the various combinations that were used, or most databases (CD-ROM and on-line) will allow you to save the search strategy to file.

Note-taking

During the course of your research project, you will read and make notes from many information sources. It is important to make accurate and clear notes so that they are legible and comprehensible when you consult them without the source in hand. It is an individual choice as to how to keep and organise the notes that you take, and may include using notebooks, reference cards, sheets or software packages.

Note-taking needs to be done systematically, and requires discipline from the start of the project. At a later stage in the project, you may wish to use the information in your writing or return to the original information source. In your notes, it should be possible to distinguish between a direct quotation, a paraphrase or summary of the original passage, and your opinions. It is also important that you can locate the notes that you have made and the items from which they were taken. Notes should be accompanied by the full bibliographic details of the item consulted. It is worthwhile making a note of sources that do not appear to be relevant when consulted as the source may become relevant at a later stage in your research, or will act as a reminder of the content of the item if you came across a reference to the same source again.

Making photocopies of relevant sections of an information source (within the copyright regulations) may be regarded as a form of note-taking. The photocopy can be used as a notebook that can be annotated with comments. Although photo-copying is an easy and, in some cases, convenient way of recording information, it has cost implications and may also result in the mindless accumulation of unassimilated pages (Berry 1994).

Referencing

It is worthwhile, at an early stage of your research project, to find out which referencing style or citation format is used by or acceptable to your organisation. The Harvard citation style, the *Publication Manual of the American Psychological Association*, and the MLA style handbook are widely used. It is important to systematically record all elements of the bibliographic information required for a citation while you have the source in hand – trying at a later stage, probably when you are writing up for the final report, to find page numbers for journal articles or imprint details of monographs that you possibly consulted elsewhere or on inter-library loan, is both difficult and time-consuming.

There are several software packages that are available for storing and managing bibliographic references and can be used to help create bibliographies in word processed documents including EndNote, Pro-Cite, Papyrus and Reference Manager.

Guides to citing references

Gibaldi, J. (1999). *MLA Handbook for Writers of Research Papers*. New York: MLA.

Li, X. and Crane, N. (1996) *Electronic Style: A Guide To Citing Electronic Information*. Westport: Meckler.

Publication Manual for the American Psychological Association. (1994) (fourth edition). Washington, DC: American Psychological Association.

References and further reading

Berry, R. (1994) The Research Project: How to Write it. London: Routledge.

Fink, A. (1998) *Conducting Research Literature Reviews: From Paper to the Internet*. London: Sage.

Gash, S. (1989) *Effective Literature Searching for Students*. Aldershot: Gower.

Jellinek, D. (1998) Official UK: The Essential Guide to Government Websites. London: Stationery Office.

Analysing data

♦ David Wilkinson

Introduction

By the time you reach this chapter you should already have your data neatly collected and piled up waiting for analysis. Therefore, by the time you get to the analysis stage, all the hard work has been done. Earlier chapters have guided you through the minefields of developing research questions, reviewing the literature, locating information and collecting data. The purpose of this chapter is to assist with interpreting and analysing the data you have collected. Data comes to us in many shapes and forms. The role of analysis is to bring data together in a meaningful way and enable us as researchers to interpret or make sense of it.

This chapter begins by outlining the importance of classifying data in order to make it ready for analysis. Essentially, two data types exist (as briefly discussed in Chapter 1) – quantitative and qualitative data. These types are detailed, and the common methods used to analyse these types of data are provided. Throughout the chapter examples are given which indicate how to present these data and the results of their analysis.

The focus in this chapter is on the data analysis methods required by those conducting research for the first time. As a result, the substance of the chapter deals with the widely used quantitative analysis methods rather than those associated with qualitative data. For those interested in qualitative research methods, the references and further reading section at the end of this chapter provides details of a number of useful texts on the subject.

Classifying data

Before analysing data, it must be classified or coded in some way. In doing this we are preparing the data for analysis. Some people refer to this as cleaning or organising data. For example, data could be organised by entering it into a computer or grouping it into batches relating to the date it was received. Another method of coding would be to convert the responses in a questionnaire into, for example, numeric form.

Examples of quantitative and qualitative data

Quantitative data
- Number of students enrolled at a college.
- Trends in sales figures.
- Imports of cars by each country in Europe.
- Number of travellers per year using a particular airport.

Qualitative data
- A particular view on euthanasia.
- Interpretation of a painting.
- The interaction of children in a playground.
- Documents tabled at a meeting.
- Minutes of a meeting.
- Film footage of a music concert.

It is important to note at this point that the analyses you can perform on your data depends upon its basic type. It could be quantitative data, for example, a collection of figures relating to the number of cars sold over a period of time. Alternatively, your data could be more qualitative in nature and consist of an oral account relating to a personal experience of the National Health Service. Both types of data require specific approaches to their analysis.

Qualitative data

In order to provide some structure and meaning to qualitative data it must be coded or cleaned in some way. For example, an interview may (and usually will) produce a great deal of information relating to given topics. How do we sort this? How are we going to compare it to other interviews? How do we draw themes from it?

> Qualitative data include observations, interviews and life history accounts. They enable the voices of those being researched to be heard. Qualitative data is usually analysed by subjecting it to some form of coding process.

The coding frame

An often-used tool to aid sorting and analysis of these kind of data is the coding frame. This technique is used in many research organisations as a way of classifying data and drawing themes from it. For example, a theme may emerge, from a number of interviews with musicians, that playing a musical instrument began as a hobby for them whilst at school. This type of response to the question: '*When did you first show an interest in music?*' could be categorised as 'school'. The number of categories or themes which may emerge from your data will depend on a number of variables such as the amount of data collected and the breadth of views.

As you begin to code your data you will discover that many categories will initially be created. However, the purpose of creating these categories is to *reduce* the data – so categories may need to be subsumed into super categories in order for the reader to digest the information quickly. As an example, statements 'A' and 'C' in the samples on page 80 could be placed in the super category of 'During time spent in education'. The number of categories will depend on the amount of data you have and the requirements of those reading the eventual report. For

---

Sample categories that may emerge from the data

Statement	Code
(A) As a child I loved to sit with the teacher at the piano and listen to her play.	Child
(B) Following a car accident I spent a great deal of time in hospital and I found music helped pass the days.	Hospital
(C) I joined a music club at college.	College

---

example, if they are concerned with detail, more categories may be necessary, whereas if they want a broad overview, fewer categories may be more appropriate.

When developing codes it may be useful to take a sample of your interviews and then develop a coding frame from them. A good yardstick is to attempt to develop a framework from approximately 20–30 per cent of your interviews. However, if this involves a great number of interviews, you may notice recurrent and similar themes emerging by transcript 7 that are not expanded upon in subsequent transcripts. If this is the case, you will need to exercise your discretion as to whether the analysis of further transcripts is appropriate.

Developing coding frames

1. Take a sample of your interviews.
2. Read through the sample transcripts several times.
3. Identify an exhaustive list of emerging themes/categories and number these.
4. Group linked categories into super-categories.
5. Create a coding frame reference by providing examples from the interviews of all your themes/categories on a separate sheet of paper.
6. Ask a colleague/friend to take your coding frame reference and the same sample of interviews and re-code the interviews.
7. Compare codings (you should attempt for over 80 per cent accuracy in your codings).
8. Re-code interviews if necessary.
9. Apply the coding frame reference to all the remaining interviews.

Although the process of categorising and coding data has traditionally been a manual process of transcribing an interview and literally cutting and pasting it into categories or chunks, it has recently become possible to perform this form of analysis using a computer. There are many excellent programs available to support this process, such as NUDIST and NVIVO, and a great deal of the administrative task of handling the data can be reduced by using them. However, researchers must be aware that these programmes *assist* the user in developing coding frames and theories about the data. They do not replace the role of theory-building – this remains the responsibility of the researcher – rather, they provide a platform for maintaining and assisting in its development.

Quantitative data

In essence, analysis of your data can occur in one of two ways. It can either be a descriptive analysis, which describes the data, or it can be an analysis that questions the data or tests hypotheses. The latter form of analysis is known as inferential analysis and usually involves subjecting your data to some form of statistical test.

> Quantitative data are those types of data that can usually be reduced to numerical form. The analysis of these data types involves manipulating them in some way and/or applying some form of statistical test.

Descriptive analysis

There are many ways to analyse quantitative data. A key concern here will be a reference to the knowledge of your audience. For example, an investigation of admissions into hospital could be conducted by collecting and presenting data on the number of admissions in a given year (Figure 6.1). However, the analysis might include a breakdown of admissions by gender and a comparison of recent years (see Figure 6.2). These data may have been collected as part of a larger research project examining the operation of Paperfield Hospital, or they could have been obtained from a nationally available database relating to hospital admissions.

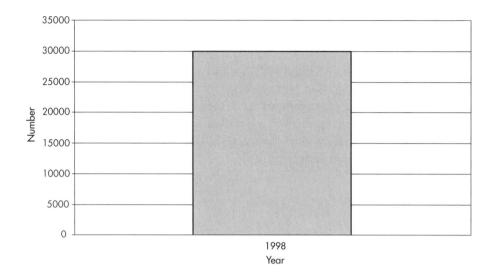

FIGURE 6.1 Number of admissions to Paperfield Hospital

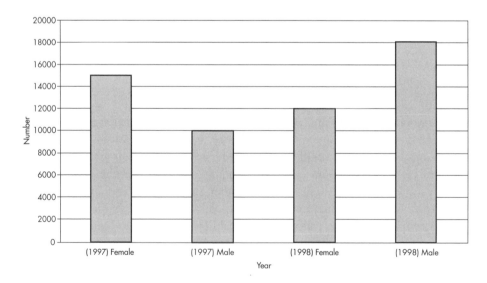

FIGURE 6.2 Number of admissions to Paperfield Hospital by gender

Variables

A variable is one of the factors in your data. For example, height, weight and test scores might be variables. Variables can be either independent or dependent. A dependent variable is one that you would expect to see change following an increase or decrease in an associated independent variable. For example, you might expect to see a change in exam results (dependent variable) following an increase in lectures attended (independent variable).

Another way of reporting or analysing these data would be to indicate the percentage of male and female admissions in the chosen years (Figures 6.3 and 6.4). This would be a useful way of showing any increase or decrease in male and female admissions.

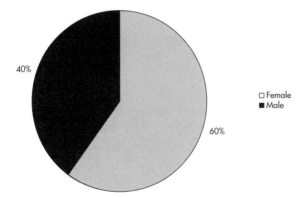

FIGURE 6.3 Number of admissions to Paperfield Hospital (1997)

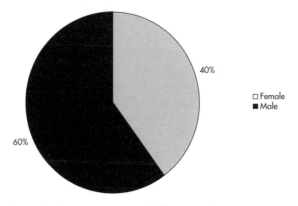

FIGURE 6.4 Number of admissions to Paperfield Hospital (1998)

Essentially, these types of interpretation or analysis provide descriptions of your data. They provide a way of reducing data into easily and quickly understood chunks. It may be that data relating to admissions is initially split by a number of factors, such as duration of admission, department admitting the patient, doctor in charge of the patient, site of admission, and so on. This may well be useful and informative, but it could confuse those reading the output of your research if they are merely concerned with the number of patients admitted. For those who are interested in the detail of the numbers admitted to hospital, you may wish to produce a separate report or a technical addition detailing the additional breakdown of the data. For example, you may wish to explore your data further to establish the ages of those admitted. Suppose that 50 women were admitted into a small department in Paperfield Hospital in 1997 and the data relating to their ages is made available to you.

What can you do with these data? When they are listed, as shown in Figure 6.5, they are difficult to interpret. You could begin by taking the data and listing the ages from the highest to the lowest. However, this would not add a great deal to the analysis of the data (although it would allow you to quickly establish the oldest and youngest female admitted). A helpful way to present the data would be to produce a 'tally chart' indicating how many times each age appears on the list (Figure 6.6).

Whilst producing a tally chart (or frequency chart as it is also known) helps you to analyse the age data, it still remains difficult to draw any useful meaning from it. Reducing the data further into larger chunks may help, and the use of age ranges may assist with this. When grouping data into ages it is acceptable to use 5 to 10 year categories (Figure 6.7).

50	49	33	38	60	63
64	70	81	45	26	20
19	45	58	56	22	33
45	47	84	30	28	29
37	42	41	62	26	30
46	48	45	39	25	66
45	50	49	33	38	60
63	64	70	81	44	26
20	19				

FIGURE 6.5 Age of women admitted to Department A in 1997

Age	19	20	22	25	26	28	29	30	33	37	38	39
Number of patients	2	2	1	1	3	1	1	2	3	1	2	1

Age	41	42	44	45	46	47	48	49	50	56	58	60
Number of patients	1	1	2	4	1	1	1	2	2	1	1	2

Age	62	63	64	66	70	81	84
Number of patients	1	2	2	1	2	2	1

FIGURE 6.6 Tally chart of ages: women admitted to Department A

Age	19–23	24–28	29–33	34–38	39–43	44–48	49–53
No.	5	5	6	3	3	9	4

Age	54–58	59–63	64–68	69–73	74–78	79–83
No.	2	5	3	2	0	3

FIGURE 6.7 Grouping of ages: women admitted to Department A

The mode, median and mean

The 'chunking' of the data now allows us to see that of the women admitted to this department, more were aged between 44 and 48 than any other grouping. This statement refers to the age range with the most occurrences. This is also known as the mode age range.

Mode

The mode of a group of data is the most frequently occurring value. For example, in the results of an examination, it might be the most often occurring grade.

If, instead, you were interested in establishing the age range that was the centre of all your ranges, this is known as the median age range. To find the median, you would list your ages from highest to lowest and count from each end until you reached the middle. In this case the median age is 45. Where there is an even number of values (ages in this case), the median is the average of the two mid-points (45+45 divided by two equals 45).

Median

The median is the value that separates the upper half of a list of values from the lower half. The median is, therefore, the mid-point in an ordered list of values.

Whilst this is a useful exercise in determining the middle value, it is still a time-consuming exercise to perform. First of all you need to rank or list your ages in order and then you must establish your middle point. Another way of calculating the middle of a set of ages (or values) is to use the mean value.

The mean, or average as it is also known, is calculated by adding together all the ages and dividing that result by the number of women admitted. Therefore, the total of all the ages is 2264 divided by the number of women admitted (50) equals 45.28. The mean, or average, age for the women admitted to this department in 1997 was 45.

The mode, median and mean are all known as measures of central tendency. They provide single values that best describes the group.

Mean

The mean is defined as the sum of the values divided by the total number of values. For example, the mean following exam results would be:

Exam result   45   67   70   55   42   78   59

Mean = 45+67+70+55+42+78+59 = 419

Divided by the number of results (7) = 59

Mean exam result = 59

Following this, you may wish to explore further the frequency of ages of those admitted. A visual way of doing this would be to develop a frequency distribution graph (Figure 6.8).

This graph shows that most of the women admitted to the department were under 46 years of age – you will notice that there is more activity in the graph between the ages of 19 and 46. This is known as a skewed distribution, whereby the results are grouped to one side of the graph. In many studies a distribution

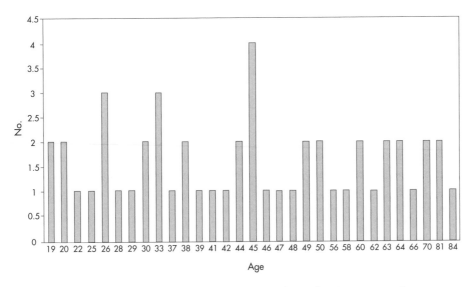

FIGURE 6.8 Frequency distribution graph: women admitted to Department A

occurs where most of the values group around the middle of the graph. This is known as a normal distribution. If this were the case you would notice that the figures for the mode, median and mean were all similar in value. As an example, you might expect a normal distribution to occur when looking at exam results of undergraduates (see Figure 6.9).

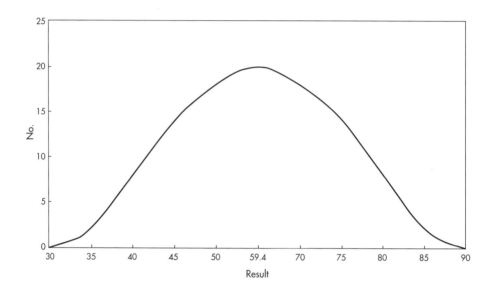

FIGURE 6.9 Graph of exam results

Standard deviation

From normally distributed data you can measure the distribution of values around the mean. Using the exam score example, this would be useful as it would allow you to establish the degree of dispersion or difference between the scores. If the standard deviation is large then the scores vary considerably, whereas if the standard deviation is small then the scores are much closer together.

The standard deviation is a key basic statistical technique, which is a requirement of many more advanced techniques. In essence, the standard deviation provides an average of all the deviations from the mean. There are a number of ways to calculate the standard deviation, one of the simplest is:

$$\text{Standard deviation} = \sqrt{\sum X^2 - \bar{X}^2}$$

Where ΣX^2 = the sum of the squared scores
$\overline{X}$ = the mean of the scores
N = the number of scores

By way of example, consider the exam results reported earlier:

Exam result	X^2
45	2025
67	4489
70	4900
55	3025
42	1764
78	6084
59	3481
$\Sigma X = 416$	$\Sigma X^2 = 25768$

$\overline{X} = 416 / 7 = 59.4$

Standard Deviation $= \sqrt{25768 / 7 - (59.4)^2} = \sqrt{153} = 12.4$

Standard Deviation = 12.4

Having established the standard deviation for the exam scores, we can see that there is some dispersion among the results. In addition, if the distributions of scores are normal (as shown in Figure 6.9), certain statements can be made about the results. In a normal distribution the range from –1 standard deviation to +1 standard deviation contains 68 per cent of the results, the range from –2 standard deviations to +2 standard deviations contains 95 per cent of the results, and the range from –3 standard deviations to +3 standard deviations contains 99 per cent of the results.

The standard deviation is a useful way of comparing across different sets of data. For example, it could be used to compare the variability in different exam results – such as Law and Accountancy – among a cohort of students. It is also used as a basis for many more detailed statistical analyses of your data (see, for example, inferential analysis on p. 94).

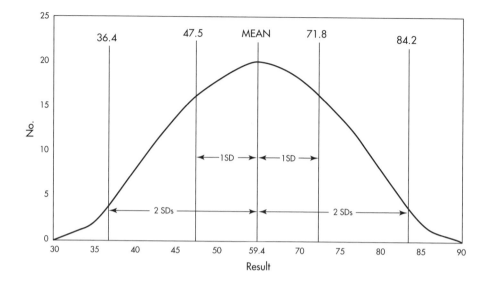

FIGURE 6.10 Graph of exam results showing standard deviation

Standard deviation

The standard deviation is a tool used to measure dispersion. The standard deviation shows the relation a set of values has to the mean. Assuming that the distribution of scores is normal, certain statements can be made about the data (69 per cent of values fall within 1 standard deviation of the mean, 95 per cent lie within 2 standard deviations of the mean, and 99 per cent lie within 3 standard deviations).

Associating data

You may find that with some of your data you wish to explore possible relationships between two different sets of data (or variables, as they are also known). This is often referred to as correlation research. There are numerous techniques available for exploring the relationships between variables. Two of the most commonly used are Pearson's Product Moment Correlation Coefficient and Spearman's Rank Order Correlation Coefficient. Both of these analyses indicate whether an association is positive (with a maximum value of +1) or negative (with a maximum value of –1). It is usually the case that scatterplots are used to show the results of the analysis.

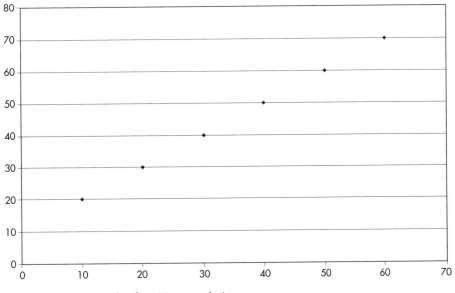

FIGURE 6.11 Example of positive correlation

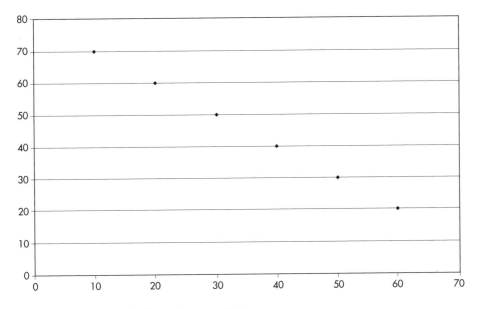

FIGURE 6.12 Example of negative correlation

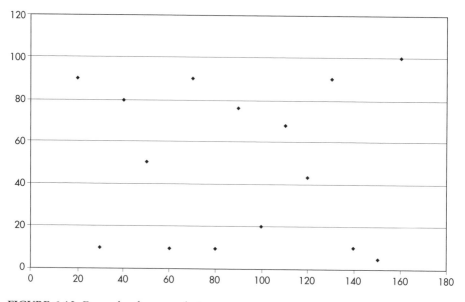

FIGURE 6.13 Example of no correlation

The detailed formula of correlation research is not discussed here, but the references and further reading section at the end of this chapter will direct you to appropriate statistical texts that will enable you to carry out a number of analyses of correlation. As an example, exam scores and number of lectures attended could be analysed for correlation. Using the Pearson Product Moment Correlation Coefficient approach (R), the analysis would take the following form, using the formula below:

$$R = \frac{\Sigma XY/N - \overline{XY}}{Sx\ Sy}$$

Where N = number of pairs of scores

ΣXY = the sum of the total of each pair of scores

$\overline{X}, \overline{Y}$ = the means of the 2 variables

Sx, Sy = the standard deviations of the 2 variables

Exam score(X)	No. of lectures attended(Y)	X^2	Y^2	XY
48	7	2304	49	336
57	11	3249	121	627
72	16	5184	256	1152
36	2	1296	4	72
$\Sigma X = 213$	$\Sigma Y = 36$	$\Sigma X^2 = 12033$	$\Sigma Y^2 = 430$	$\Sigma XY = 2187$

$$\overline{X} = \frac{\Sigma X}{N} = \frac{213}{4} = 53.25$$

$$\overline{Y} = \frac{\Sigma Y}{N} = \frac{36}{4} = 9$$

$$Sx = \sqrt{\frac{\Sigma X^2}{N} - \overline{X}^2} = \sqrt{\frac{12033}{4} - 2835} = 13.16$$

$$Sy = \sqrt{\frac{\Sigma Y^2}{N} - \overline{Y}^2} = \sqrt{\frac{430}{4} - 81} = 5.14$$

$$R = \frac{\Sigma XY / N - XY}{Sx \ Sy} = \frac{2187 / 4 - (53.25)(9)}{(13.16)\ (5.14)}$$

$$R = 0.99$$

This indicates that there is a strong positive correlation between these two variables. However, you must take care when performing correlation analysis on your data. The appearance of a relationship does not necessarily mean one exists – it does not indicate causation. In other words, correlation does not prove that one variable causes another to alter in value.

A descriptive analysis or report of your data is a useful way of introducing the data to the reader. From a general analysis you can move on to a more detailed examination of your data (if this is appropriate, given the requirements of the reader or user of your research). Questions posed here may include: '*What are the data saying?*' and '*What do the data mean?*' Interpreting or questioning your data in this way often leads to inferentially analysing your data.

Inferential analysis

An inferential analysis of your data assists you in making conclusions about the data by performing certain operations on it. With inferential analysis you are inferring from your sample data (for example, the exam scores) what the population scores are (say, the scores for an entire group of undergraduates).

Sample

A sample is a selection which is taken from a group; it is usually considered to be representative of that group. As a result, the findings from the sample can be generalised back to the group.

Population

A population is a group who share the same characteristics. For example, a population could be members of a club, nurses, students or children.

The major difference between inferential analysis and descriptive analysis is that with descriptive techniques you are merely describing the data as it is represented to you. With inferential analysis, you test or perform some operation on the data in order to make conclusions about it.

Statistical significance

One popular method of inferential analysis is to make judgements of the probability that the difference in, say, the mean scores in a law exam for a sample of male and female students is one that is representative of all male and female students on the law programme; or whether it is down to chance. In this way, we are said to be testing the significance of the difference in exam scores.

In statistical terms, when we test for significance we must first make a statement or hypothesis about the data. For example, the hypothesis for the exam score instance could be: *'There is no significant difference in male and female exam scores'*. This statement is known as a non-directional hypothesis because it merely puts forward that no difference exists. The statistical tests to perform on this type

Statistical significance

Statistical significance refers to how much, for example, exam results for a group of students could be down to chance alone. If the results cannot be explained by chance, it is assumed that another factor, such as number of lectures attended, had an impact on the results. One of two significance levels are usually applied when testing for statistical significance – 0.05 and 0.01. These levels indicate degrees of confidence in the assumption that chance was not the cause. Whilst 0.01 is the stricter of the degrees, both can be understood as producing statistically significant results.

of hypothesis are called two-tailed tests. However, if the hypothesis were stated as: '*males perform better than females in exams*' then the hypothesis becomes directional, and a one-tailed test is required. The requirements of a one-tailed test are more strict than those for a two-tailed test, as the latter is only concerned with proving a difference exists, while the former is concerned with exploring who the difference favours.

Hypothesis

An hypothesis is a proposition or statement you wish to test with your data. They are commonly referred to as null hypotheses. These are negative statements which have to be disproved in order validate the statement made.

There are a number of statistical tests available to researchers when exploring hypotheses. These include the t-test, Analysis of Variance (ANOVA), and the Analysis of Covariance (ANCOVA). These more advanced statistical techniques are explored in traditional statistical texts and not detailed here. Those who are interested in developing a more thorough understanding of such methods may care to consult the references and further reading section at the end of this chapter.

Reporting the analysis of data

As this chapter has shown, data can be presented in a variety of ways. When you report your data it will be in one of two main forms: a table or a chart/figure.

Tables often reproduce raw data. They should be clear and uncluttered. In research reports, tables are often used to present findings, emphasise a point made in the text or act as the starting point for a discussion or analysis of some aspect of the data. Even if your report has only one table, it should be clearly labelled with a title and reference number. Some organisations and institutions have a particular 'house style' for the presentation of data, so you may need to check this.

Charts or figures are more graphical representations of your data or the results of some analysis of it. These presentational tools also require careful and clear labelling. Presenting your data as a figure or chart may include constructing a histogram, bar chart or pie chart of your data. These, as shown earlier, are often used to present descriptive analyses of your data. More complex analyses of your data, such as an exploration of correlation, are best presented as scatterplots or line graphs.

Tips for presenting data

- Remind the reader of the research question or questions when presenting data. This helps provide focus.
- Move from the general to the specific. For example, indicate general findings before moving on to the more specific and detailed elements.
- Keep linked data together in your report and deal with them in one chapter or section if possible. This aids the flow and structure of your report.
- Keep tables and figures simple! Any detail should be provided in an accompanying key, or in an appendix at the back of the report.

References and further reading

*Bryman, A. (1988) *Quantity and Quality in Social Research*. London: Routledge.

Clegg, F. (1982) *Simple Statistics: A Course Book for the Social Sciences*. Cambridge: Cambridge University Press.

Cohen, L. and Holliday, M. (1996) *Practical Statistics for Students*. London: Paul Chapman Publishing.

*Fielding, N. G. and Lee, R. M. (1998) *Computer Analysis and Qualitative Research*. London: Sage.

*Miles, M. B. and Huberman, A. M. (1994) *Qualitative Data Analysis: An Expanded Sourcebook* (second edition). London: Sage.

*Tesch, R. (1990) *Qualitative Research: Analysis Types and Software Tools*. London: Falmer Press.

Wright, D. B. (1989) *Understanding Statistics: An Introduction for the Social Sciences*. London: Sage.

(*Of particular relevance to those interested in exploring qualitative research methods)

Chapter 7

Completing the research project

♦ Christine Gough

The process of writing up

The completion stage of a research project focuses on the writing-up process. Many people who undertake research find the prospect of writing very daunting. This is not just confined to new researchers. Even people with many years of research experience can lack confidence. Research writing has been termed '*one of the most difficult tasks that human beings have set themselves*' (Orna and Stevens 1995: 162). This is a statement that I am sure many of us have identified with when faced with that looming essay or report deadline.

However, like it or not, writing remains the main way to communicate research. Whatever context you are researching in, some form of written output will be required. For example, in education, it might be a dissertation or thesis. In a work context, it might be a report. For that reason this chapter has been written to be applicable in whatever research setting you may find yourself.

In a lot of the 'how to do literature' on research, there is limited attention given to advice on the writing itself. However, as much as people dread writing, they don't want to waste valuable time reading about how to do it. This chapter offers a concise and practical approach to the process of writing, drawing on some of the literature as well as using my and others' experiences. I argue that if you adopt a more systematic approach to writing, then it doesn't have to be the most dreaded task of the research process. Many researchers muddle through for years in a disorganised way making writing more difficult than it has to be.

This chapter is split into six sections. The first section will deal with the process aspect of writing up, looking at motivational problems, problems in starting, the 'when' issue, organising and coding sources, time management and general guidelines for the writing process. Section two deals with issues relating to targeting an audience, focusing particularly on conventions and content. Then section three deals with writing style, referencing and how you should structure your findings. Section four considers how to schedule for feedback and respond to it. Then, for when the bulk of the writing is done, section five deals with revisions and in particular, editing and evaluating your writing. The final section deals with what happens once you have finished writing, i.e. submission for assessment or publication or both. Whilst there is no substitute for experience, the following sections will give you useful pointers to guide you into the ways of writing that work best for you.

Motivation

The first question is when should writing begin? Many researchers mistakenly think that the report should be written up after all of the data have been collected and analysed, i.e. at the end of the research. Indeed placing the writing up section at the end in much of the literature on research processes (as is the case here!) would imply that this should be the case. That is why I take this opportunity now to stress that it is important to begin writing early on in the research project. As Blaxter et al. (1996: 208–9) point out:

> Writing up your research should start early and become a regular and continuing activity. It is also likely to be an iterative or cyclical process. That is, you will draft a section or chapter, then move on to some other activity,

and return one or more times to redraft your original version. This is partly because as the totality of the research thesis or report takes shape, what you have written in subsequent sections affects what you wrote earlier and necessitates changes in it. It is also the case that as your research proceeds you find out more, read more, and change your mind about some things.

However, this is all well and good, but, as mentioned in the introduction, many people find writing difficult. Many experience motivational problems relating to starting writing, such as lack of confidence, lead to researchers putting things off. Also, a lot of new researchers grossly underestimate the length of time that is necessary for writing, which can lead to problems with deadlines and the quality of reports due to cramming at the end. This section will deal with both of these problems.

First, the problem of 'putting things off'. Blaxter et al. (1996) deal with this issue in more detail, but in a lot of cases, problems relating to this seem to be due to a lack of confidence because people put pressure on themselves to get it perfect first time. Also, it can be due to a lack of focus and knowledge of what is expected of you. That is why it is important to begin writing early on, otherwise you are faced with that dreaded task at the end of the project. So, allocate plenty of time for it in your workplan because this will reduce the amount of stress that you put yourself under. The main advice from the texts is to get something down on paper that you know will be of use to you in some kind of thematic form. Even the most experienced of researchers don't come up with the ideal version first time round. If you schedule writing into your workplan regularly, then it will gradually get easier.

Tips for getting started

Write what is fact and then build on that. One researcher I know said that when having problems writing a book it is a good idea to get your structure laid out and then write what you know without the aid of notes, literature, and so on, and then build from that. This can help you to get the main themes down on paper and develop linkages.

Another useful idea to get you focused is to decide on the number of words you will devote to each section based on the report's word limit. However, here there are some factors to consider, which are summarised by Denscombe (1998: 235) as follows:

When a word count becomes crucial, such as is often the case with academic dissertations, it is worth noting that the total normally includes only those sections from the introduction to the conclusions/recommendations. References, appendices and indexes are not normally included, nor is the initial material before the introduction, such as the contents page, preface, etc. It is always worth checking, however, that this convention applies in each specific instance when submitting a research report.

The rest of this section offers guidelines for organising your information for writing and time management.

Organising

Instead of using the 'muddle through' approach that I used for years, I have adopted a system for writing adapted from the 'design approach' of Orna and Stevens (1995). This emphasises the importance of organising your information closely in line with the structure of your report before writing. Many of the research process books pay little attention to how critical it is to organise your information. I definitely learned the hard way over the years, until I started using this simple but effective approach. Critics would say that it stunts creativity; however, this approach arranges your sources, data and information in such a way that you can concentrate your energies on writing. Whether writing for an essay, journal, book, or report, this method can be applied to all types of writing outputs. I am not suggesting that you follow this method rigidly, but think of it as a framework that you can adapt to your own needs. Even for those who actually like writing, this method can help improve the quality of your output. Also, it can be applied to either a manual or computer database of sources. This approach consists of the following stages:

Stage 1 First, write a draft contents list and break it down into chapters or sections, or both. Then label your sources, data and any other information in line with these. This labelling will be done continuously throughout the whole process as you build up more references and data.

Stage 2 Think of your report as a whole, and mark out the sequence of ideas and linkages between them. If it's useful, draw a diagram showing these linkages.

Stage 3 Within each chapter or section, decide on the themes, draw links and number the themes to show the order that they will be placed in. Then add these themes to your contents list. Next, code each theme with a different shape and colour and mark your sources accordingly. Then pile them in the relevant order for each chapter.

Stage 4 You can start writing after stage 3, but if the report is particularly lengthy, it can be useful to sketch the framework of what you are going to write in the form of double page spreads. This provides a useful structure to write into and can aid with the logic and flow of your argument.

Stage 5   Writing. It wastes time to write in a less focused way, hoping that something will come together. Even after these stages it is unlikely that you will be able to write the perfect version of your report the first time round. Decide what you want to say briefly under each section or heading and then build up the detail gradually from that. Writing is a process of progressive refining and you should not underestimate the time it takes. Also, there is no set way to sequence your argument, so you have to choose the structure, linkages and cross-referencing that work best for each report.

A system for writing up research

1   Draft the content
2   Sequence the ideas
3   Develop the themes
4   Devise a detailed writing framework
5   Begin the write-up

Developed from Orna and Stevens (1995)

Time management

Having established an approach to writing, discipline has to come into play in order to manage your study time efficiently and effectively and thus meet the deadlines.

Break down your writing into key stages according to, say, particular themes or sections and then set targets for each, allotting a specific amount of time for each task. See how much you get written within this writing plan and then you can adjust it accordingly. This method gives you more focus – it is surprising how much more you get done if you have set time frames to focus on. Of course, if you feel that you can add a lot more within each session then do so. Set time frames are useful for people who are having problems with discipline and focus. In terms of appropriate time allocations, these are difficult to gauge at first but they will be easier to estimate with practice when you get more of a feel for your pace of writing.

If you are writing the report jointly, it should be made clear early on in the research who will contribute to each chapter or section. Then, relevant deadlines can be set to increase the chances of you all completing your tasks at the same time so that the report can be pulled together without major delays. Therefore, it is useful to develop a writing workplan for the project.

Time-saving tips

1   First, make sure that you work in a place where distractions can be kept to a minimum because they reduce flow and efficiency in your writing. If you think that interruptions will be inevitable then write a more detailed plan of key tasks that you have to do within each writing session. Therefore you can keep track of what you are doing.
2   Write regularly so that you gain momentum – it will get easier and quicker with practice.
3   Consider the quality of time and effort that you are putting in – keep focused – and don't kid yourself that because you have been sitting at your desk or computer for 6 hours that you have achieved a lot. Keep reviewing the outputs of your study sessions.
4   Do the more difficult subjects or tasks at the time of day that you know you work best. For some this is in the morning. A lot of my ideas unfortunately tend to flow most rapidly in the early hours of the morning!
5   Another time-saving tip, if you have access to a PC or word processor, is to write the bulk of your work at the computer. This will save a lot of time compared to writing hand-written notes and then typing them in word for word. This may seem strange at first, but not only will it save time but also mean that you can keep a closer eye on the word limits and cut and paste sections easily.

Whilst acknowledging that drafting and redrafting will play a part, aim to get each section to a good standard first time. It is always worth trying to produce the final version at the first attempt. To write with the idea that what is written will be redrafted encourages a degree of carelessness, which can produce drafts that require complete revision. On the other hand if you aim to get it right first time, there is every chance that all that will be required is minor amendment. This is as much an attitude of mind as a matter of style.

Targeting your audience

The audience for a particular research project will differ according to the subject matter. As Denscombe (1998: 227) points out, 'there is no single set of rules and guidelines for writing up research which covers all situations and provides a universally accepted convention'. Therefore, whatever written output you are producing, you need to tailor it to the appropriate conventions and needs of potential readers.

So, very simply, think about who the report is for and what you are seeking to achieve by reporting to them. Also, think about what the audience already knows and what they need to know. As a writer you must find out what types of reader will be receiving your output and what they will be using it for. For example, you might need to consider whether they are academic or practitioner, lay or professional. Also, you might have to produce more than one report in order to cater for different groups. For example, one for the client and one for the more general reader. You will also need to consider how your written output will be used, for example, as a reference to make recommendations, to provide an overview of a subject or issue, to provide data for further use, to describe or to be critical.

The type of project and the target audience will determine the format and content of the report. For example, workplace reports may be short and less detailed, whereas academic reports are often complex and lengthy. It is usually the case that at degree level the examiners assess a dissertation or thesis according to the value of the research questions posed. In essence they decide (a) whether the questions are good ones (have they been answered already elsewhere? Are they useful question to work on?); (b) whether the student adequately answered the questions posed; and (c) whether the student made an adequate contribution to knowledge.

In addition to the above essential elements, there are usually conventions for writing and/or presentation that you need to adhere to. For example, a university, journal or institution may set out requirements in relation to length, essential information, referencing, and layout. This is discussed in the next section.

Submitting to a journal or other publication

When submitting a research paper to a journal, submission guidelines are often supplied at the back of the publication (usually on the inside of the back cover). The explosion of research-paper submissions has led to many journal editors strictly adhering to these guidelines. I know of many manuscripts or papers that have been returned to novice researchers for not complying (often to the letter) with submission requirements. The requirements can differ considerably from journal to journal, but usually consist of two elements – presentation and general content.

Example presentation requirements for a journal

♦ The paper should be printed on A4 size sheets of paper.
♦ The paper should be double-line spaced with wide margins on all sides (this enables editors to make comments on your paper as they read it).
♦ The typeface should be at least 10 point in size and in a generally recognised font such as Times New Roman.
♦ Three copies of the paper should be supplied along with an electronic version (on disk) in a generally recognised format such as Word or WordPerfect.

Example general content requirements for a journal

♦ The name of the paper.
♦ The author's name (and usually the place where the research was conducted).
♦ An abstract of the paper (usually restricted to between 200 to 600 words).
♦ The paper itself.

Content

No matter what type of report or audience you are targeting, it is usual to include ideas and information on:

Purpose	Here you want to say why the work was done and give some background to the study. Also, this part should include a statement of aims and objectives.
How the research was done	Here you should describe how the work was done with a discussion and justification of the methods used. Also, you should highlight any problems that were experienced during the research.
Presenting the findings	Here you need to detail the results.
Discuss and analyse findings	Here you interpret the results and discuss their significance.

Reach conclusions   Here you make conclusions from the analysis and, depending on the type of report, make recommendations.

Style of the report

Style relates to the way you write in relation to factors such as detail, complexity, language, terminology and references, and is a key ingredient to ensuring the quality of a report.

Whatever the written output required you should aim for clarity in order to avoid confusion and ambiguity for the reader. Therefore, you should pay particular attention to the length of sentences and paragraphs, and also vocabulary. Also use language that makes the report interesting to read.

Try to mix and match the length of sentences because this makes for a more interesting read. However, be careful not to put in sentences that are too long because they may be less easy to understand and could make it hard work for the reader. Also, break up lengthy pages of text with headings and bullet points; however, be aware that certain conventions might not accept this.

Don't use long and complex words for the sake of it. Short and simple words are better unless the conventions or the field you are working in particularly require these. However, consider the tone of your writing. Depending on your audience, you need to take care not to be patronising. At the same time you have to be cautious in assuming certain things are self-evident. This is particularly important in the use of terminology.

Also, take extra care with punctuation. Lots of people find anything beyond commas, full stops and brackets too much. Dashes can be useful but should be used so as not to halt the flow of the report.

When developing an argument that is complex, break it up into separate parts and create linkages to make it easier for the reader to follow.

Another important factor to consider is whether to write using a passive or active voice. A passive voice could be used to de-personalise the research – which would be useful if confidential data were consulted. An example would be *'The conclusion that some managers receive more than others was indicated by information relating to salary levels'*. However, the active voice provides more information and can aid clarity. An example would be *'Salary information indicates that some managers receive more than others'*.

Whatever style you use the important thing is to be consistent.

Finally, it is generally accepted that research reports should be written in a non-discriminatory way, that is, in such a way that does not denigrate or exclude particular groups of people on the basis of what may be fairly arbitrary characteristics like sex, race, religion, physical and mental abilities or sexual orientation.

Structure of the report

This section offers general guidelines on structure which can be adapted depending on the requirements of your audience, and the nature, detail and context of the research being undertaken.

Building on the recommendations from the last section, this part will offer a detailed breakdown of how a report should be structured. A short paragraph for each heading will be provided. This section builds on Denscombe's (1998) comprehensive list of sections which follows the academic model. He divides the structure of a report into the preliminary part, the main text and the end matter. The headings under each can be used in line with the requirements of your report.

Preliminary part

Title	This should reflect the contents of the report but has to be brief. Some researchers find it necessary to include a sub-heading in order to give more detail.
Abstract	This is a one page summary of the work of approximately 250–300 words. This should give the broad aims of the work and conclusions. People often only read this to see if the report will be of any use and so it needs to be written well.
List of contents	List sections or, if it is a lengthy report, each chapter and section. Also, the appropriate page numbers should be given.
Lists of figures and tables	On the figures/tables themselves make sure you acknowledge the sources, and label axes on graphs, etc. correctly.
Preface	This is a personal statement from the author who mentions something about the events leading up to the study and the significance of it.
Acknowledgements	Here acknowledge the people who have supported you during the research. Also acknowledge those people or organisations that have cooperated with it.
Abbreviations	Here provide a list of the full version of each one.

The main text

Introduction	Here give some background to the study and outline the purpose. Then aims, objectives and hypotheses should be set out along with an indication of the scope of the project and the main gaps in knowledge that will be addressed.
Literature review	This should cover background theory/knowledge, key concepts and definitions, and will show how the research fits in with these. However, it should not be an account of everything that you have read which vaguely relates to the research. You have to be selective here.
Methods	This should show how the methods were used to address each of the objectives. Therefore, it should include a justification of the overall research design and methods – for example, a case study or survey. Also which type of instruments were used to gather the data – questionnaire, interview, etc. In addition, what type of data where gathered – quantitative, qualitative or both?
	If it is a survey, you should cover things like the population surveyed and the sample size. If a case study, justify your selection and how you gained access, and say who was involved.
	If appropriate, you should give an account of the research at each stage and mention any problems that may have affected the results.
	Finally, you should say how the data were analysed, be it statistically or otherwise.
	Also acknowledge the limitations of the research in relation to such things as time constraints and accuracy.
Results	Here you should set out the results in an organised way – for example, in relation to a particular theme or issue. The more academic the report, the more specific these should be.
Analysis and discussion	This should interpret the results and highlight the most significant ones and perhaps deduce things from them. Here you discuss the findings in relation to the background theories and knowledge and the original aims of the project.

Some researchers prefer to have the results, analysis and discussion as one section because they think that it gives a more rounded summary of the research. This is matter of taste and convention.

Conclusions and recommendations

Here the researcher needs to assess the extent to which the original goals of the study have been met. Also, it will reflect on the methods used. It might recommend action or show how it has increased our understanding. Consider the questions remaining or generated by the research and recommend further research. It is important, at these stages, to draw together the threads of the research in order to arrive at some general conclusion and, perhaps to suggest some way forward. Attempt to make them positive and constructive.

The end matter

Appendices

Here you should include anything that might interrupt the flow of the arguments in the report. Material included here is generally too detailed for inclusion in the main report, but should be available for examination by readers to show them the material or instruments you have used, for example questionnaires and interview schedules.

References

This should be an alphabetical list of all of the authors cited or referred to in the text. It should not be confused with a bibliography, which is a list of everything that you have read during the study. The Harvard System is the most widely used. Within this system the ideas of the author are referred to in summary or by direct quotation. Then in the back of the report, the authors or organisation are listed in alphabetical order. The next section deals with this in more detail.

References

The following are examples of how to reference different works.

> ## What should your reference include?
>
> ◆ The surname and initial of each author, editor, or the name of the institution.
> ◆ Date of publication.
> ◆ The title, including any sub-titles.
> ◆ The name of the journal if applicable (should also include the volume, number and page numbers).
> ◆ Place of publication.
> ◆ The publisher.
> ◆ The edition (only if it is a second, third or fourth edition, etc.).

A BOOK OR REPORT

Bell, J. (1993) *Doing Your Research Project: A Guide for First-time Researchers in Education and Social Science*. Buckingham: Open University Press. Second Edition.

A JOURNAL

Kershaw, B. (1990) Clinical credibility and nurse teachers. *Nursing Standard* 4(51): 46–7.

AN ORGANISATION OR INSTITUTION

United Kingdom Central Council for Nursing, Midwifery and Health Visiting (1990) *The Report of the Post Registration Education and Practice Project*. London: UKCC.

CHAPTERS IN BOOKS

Tierney, A. (1996) Reporting and Disseminating Research, in D. F. S. Cormack (ed.) *The Research Process in Nursing* (third edition). Oxon: Blackwell Science. pp. 373–385.

PAPERS IN PUBLISHED PROCEEDINGS OF CONFERENCES

Gough, C. (1998) *Organisational Effectiveness: Lessons from the Public Sector*, in Proceedings of the Organisational Effectiveness Annual One Day Conference, 17 June, Edge Hill University College, Lancashire. pp. 56–64.

UNPUBLISHED PAPERS

Wilkinson, D. (1998) Access in the context of lifelong learning. Unpublished manuscript.

THESES

Stoney, C. (1996) Strategic Management in Local Government. Unpublished Ph.D. thesis, Leeds Metropolitan University.

Obtaining and acting on feedback

The best way to improve and develop your writing is to be willing to accept criticism either formally or informally. For obvious reasons people feel uneasy with this but the best thing to do is to see it as a positive opportunity to learn. Particularly for a large-scale project, it is important to schedule for feedback in your workplan at key stages, say after each chapter. Without the discipline from this activity, the writing can drift on for longer than it has to.

So, in the academic or work context you would arrange to meet with your supervisor or manager. Also, you could present a working paper at a seminar or conference, which can at first be very daunting but can be very rewarding. Also, it can be good for motivation and encourages you to focus your writing.

If the work is commissioned by another organisation, it can vary as to whether they want you to give feedback on the progress of the work at intervals, say via an interim report or upon completion of the project. If the latter is the case it would be advisable for you to arrange to meet with the client when you have some form of draft so that you can be sure that their requirements are being met. This could save time at the end and avoid the problem of the report being thrown back at the end for major changes.

Whatever the research context, make sure that you meet with your supervisor, manager or client before the final draft stage to ensure that you have fulfilled the requirements and addressed any problem areas.

If you are new to research it is particularly important that you get feedback in relation to the ethical standards in your field. This is to ensure that you have taken the necessary precautions to ensure anonymity and confidentiality. In the case of a large-scale survey it would be relatively easy to ensure this, but in case study or small-scale research it may be more difficult to de-personalise comments or responses. In the nursing field, much of the ethical debate centres on the need to protect the individual from harm. For more on this consult McHaffie (1996).

Once you have received feedback, you must consider whether your report needs to be adjusted at all. Also, it is worth evaluating the criticisms and ensure that they were made for all the right reasons.

Revising the report

Once you have made the necessary adjustments from the feedback you need to edit and evaluate your work.

Bell (1993: 160–1) argues for the need for revision.

> One problem about spending so much time on the original draft (the most difficult part of the writing stage) is that parts of it may seem right simply because they have been read so often. Another is that you may be so familiar with the subject that you assume something is understandable to the reader when it is not. Time will give you a better perspective on your writing, so you should put the script aside – for several days – so that you can return to it with a more critical eye. This will help you to identify repetitive passages, errors of expression and lack of clarity.

Therefore, because there is a tendency to become immersed in your writing it is important to take a break from your writing for a day or two in order to be able to edit and evaluate your work effectively.

Revision/editing checklist

- Check for accuracy in spelling, referencing, quotations, grammar and punctuation.
- Check that your arguments are clear with logic and flow and that any headings and sub-headings are used appropriately.
- Test for readability – this will be affected by the sentence and paragraph length and links between sections and chapters.
- Make sure that the layout, presentation and referencing style meets with the appropriate conventions.
- In the literature review assess whether an adequate number and type of sources have been included – for example, between academic and practitioner. Also ensure there is a balance in articles from books, journals and other sources.

(continued)

- ◆ Have the methods and analysis techniques been adequately justified? Also, are the data reliable?
- ◆ Ensure that the findings are clearly presented and that the discussion is analytical and critical and not just a mere description.
- ◆ Also ask yourself: Have the original objectives been achieved? If applicable, have hypotheses been proved or not?
- ◆ Make sure that your conclusions are based on evidence from your findings.
- ◆ Is the layout and style consistent?

Working through the revision checklist can be helpful if you are experiencing problems finishing off. A common reason for delaying this is that you don't think that your work is good enough. Once you are satisfied that all of these points have been met, then proof-read the final draft. It is useful to do this by reading out loud.

Submission and publication

Submission

Before you submit your work, you need to check that you have met the appropriate presentation requirements, such as margin sizes, line spacing, paper size, number of copies, and whether it needs to be bound or not.

In the academic setting it is likely that you will be assessed internally by the relevant tutors or committee. However, if you go for a higher degree like an M.Phil. or Ph.D., an external examiner will assess you. In the workplace, senior management or the board who requested the work may assess you. In either case you may be requested to a do a presentation and in the academic context, an oral examination.

There is no such thing as a standard oral examination or presentation. For either it is important to prepare and 'perhaps the best mental preparation of all is for students to be in a position to exploit the strengths of their writing and to pre-empt criticism of its weaknesses' (Sharp and Howard 1996: 221). You need to demonstrate a clear grasp of the research context, what your research has contributed to the problem and any limitations. If you feel particularly apprehensive about doing presentations, then there are plenty of guides to help build your confidence. One that I have found particularly useful is *Confident Speaking: How to Communicate Effectively Using the Power Talk System* by Godefroy and Barrat (1990).

Now for the outcome of your assessment. In the work context the outcome of the assessment process will be to have the work accepted or referred for minor modifications. However, in the academic context, it is most likely that your work will be passed with or without a request for alterations. The two most common referral cases are for plagiarism or for referral for a lower qualification if the examiners think that you have not achieved the appropriate level.

Plagiarism

Plagiarism is any attempt to mislead by passing off the ideas or work of others as your own. Therefore you must ensure that any quotations, paraphrasing or citations are fully acknowledged.

If you feel that you have been treated unfairly with your work you can go through the relevant appeals process. If you are a student, for example, you will be able to go through the relevant Student Grievance procedure and get support from the Students' Union complaints procedure at your institution. However, in most cases, referrals require minor modifications and are considered part and parcel of the research process, so you should not feel too disappointed if your work requires it.

Publication

Once your work is completed and accepted you may decide to publish in order to spread the word more widely in the public arena and to improve your standing in your own research community. It is also a useful tool for promotion, job-seeking and networking with others in your research field. Seeing your name in print can give you a great sense of satisfaction after all the labours of your research. In nursing, as well as many other fields, publishing is particularly important. This is emphasised by Tierney (1996: 377):

> Research is still a relatively recent development in nursing and much of the work is still in the form of small-scale, one-off studies. Further research will be all the more useful if it builds on studies previously undertaken and, for this to be done, there needs to be access to earlier work in published form. It is not only intending researchers who need access to this material. Students and teachers need it too if research is to be incorporated into nurse education.

You could aim to publish a book, a review article or a monograph. However, the most popular is in the learned journal. For general readership in the area of nursing, it may be useful to publish in the *Nursing Standard* or *Nursing Times*. Or if you are writing for a specific audience, choose something such as *Cancer Nursing* or *Journal of Clinical Nursing*. The best thing to do is to scan the journals in your library and examine the writing style used by contributors. Also, get a sense of what the top journals are in your field. Your library should be able to assist with this by providing you with the names of the most popular titles.

When targeting aim for the top journals first, it is worth having a go two or three times before you opt for a lower ranking one. However, at the same time, the lower ranking journals are not to be underestimated because they can reach a wide audience. Also aim for a journal that has a record for publishing in your specialist area – this might increase your chances. Always be aware of the different styles of journals. Some require a lot of theory, others are happy with a brief overview of the literature before discussion of your findings. You could also target an electronic journal via the Internet, which is becoming an increasingly popular option. The advantage of this is that the publication process is a lot quicker.

Know how to pitch the tone of the article. For example, a journal for practitioners and academics will be lighter in tone than a purely academic one. Additionally, don't waffle. Instead, make the article interesting by using lively vocabulary. Be innovative with your title and make it an eyecatcher.

A lot of people only read the introduction and conclusion, so make sure that these are well written. A researcher colleague once suggested that his students should read only the emboldened parts of an article, as these were the most important parts. However, I wouldn't suggest such a minimalist approach!

Finally don't be intimidated or put off by the prospect of publishing – it is not just confined to those natural intellectuals in the great heights of academia. In fact, these people are the exception rather than the rule in the publishing arena. So have a go and believe that the product of your hard labours is worthy of publishing.

Summary checklist for writing-up

♦ Begin writing early on in the research project.
♦ Write regularly – it will gradually get easier and quicker.
♦ Tailor your writing to the appropriate needs of the audience.
♦ Style: aim for clarity and consistency.
♦ Avoid plagiarism through rigorous referencing.

- ◆ Be willing to accept criticism – it is a positive opportunity to learn.
- ◆ Take a break from your writing before revision and editing.
- ◆ Before submission, check that the appropriate presentation requirements have been met.
- ◆ Have a go at publishing – it is not confined to the heights of academia.
- ◆ Above all, make sure that your report meets the original research aims. In areas where this may not have been possible, justify appropriately.

References and further reading

Bell, J. (1993) *Doing Your Research Project: A Guide for First-time Researchers in Education and Social Science* (second edition). Buckingham: Open University Press.

Blaxter, L., Hughes, C. and Tight, M. (1996) *How to Research*. Buckingham: Open University Press.

Denscombe, M. (1998) *The Good Researcher Guide for Small-scale Social Research Projects*. Buckingham: Open University Press.

Godefroy, C. H. and Barrat, S. (1990) *Confident Speaking: How to Communicate Effectively Using The Power Talk System*. London: Piatkus.

McHaffie, H. E. (1996) Ethical issues in nursing research. In D. F. S.Cormack (ed.) *The Research Process in Nursing* (third edition). Oxford: Blackwell Science.

Orna, E. and Stevens, G. (1995) *Managing Information for Research*, Buckingham: Open University Press.

Sharp, J. A. and Howard, K. (1996) *The Management of a Student Research Project* (second edition). Aldershot. Gower.

Tierney, A. (1996) Reporting and Disseminating Research, in D. F. S. Cormack (ed.) *The Research Process in Nursing* (third edition). Oxford: Blackwell Science.

Chapter 8

Researching in schools

Case studies based on three research projects

♦ Jane Lovey

This chapter covers the following

Introduction: the case studies

All three of these projects were undertaken during the 1990s:

1   A study to establish beneficial strategies for the education of students who had been excluded from school in Key Stage 4.
2   A project to identify indicators of effective in-class support for special educational needs.
3   Exploration of the effects of adult attribution on children's problematic classroom behaviour.

The 1990s were a time of great change in schools. Schools had either chosen or been coerced into having much more responsibility for the way they were funded. Headteachers were in a position where they were expected to take on much of the work of a manager of a company, a company accountable to the public for its product and its ability to work within increasing financial restraints. However, this financial autonomy was accompanied by far more control from the government in matters that had previously been regarded as the preserve of those trained to teach, and to lead teachers. Not only was a National Curriculum imposed on the schools, with a system of assessment that was to dominate the school year, but schools were ranked in order of success in what became known as league tables.

Whilst these changes were happening within schools there were, and still are, constant news items on failing teachers, a growing minority of unruly, often illiterate pupils, and mounting exclusions from school. Not surprisingly, teacher moral hit a new low, and those headteachers who had missed the opportunity for early retirement, available at the beginning of the decade, often developed the feeling of being totally embattled and beleaguered.

It is against this background that more and more research projects in education have been undertaken by the growing undergraduate population, practising teachers studying for Masters' degrees and a growing number of Doctorate students. It is, therefore, not surprising that professional researchers have to approach projects that involve schools with greater and greater circumspection.

As a teacher who has come to a career as a contract researcher after 22 years in classrooms, I feel that it is important to understand how it feels to be on the other end of school research. Educational or social research is essentially a parasitic occupation. We feed off our subjects, and without willing heads, teachers, parents and, to a certain extent, children, we cannot undertake our research. No one would attempt to research a distant, isolated civilisation without studying the history of the people, finding out something about the customs and beliefs of the people, and arming themselves with good maps, and perhaps some gifts. The research interview is a gift (Limerick et al. 1997). This must be remembered and one needs to consider carefully what, if anything, those who participate in our research, are going to receive in return.

It is necessary to bear all this in mind before writing the proposal.

Developing workable research proposals

It is important to think carefully about how much of the headteacher's time, and individual teachers' time is going to be needed to realise the project. The only way to find out how schools really operate, and how they affect, or are affected by, the pupils within them, is to go in and observe and interview. This will initially involve the head either spending time talking to the researcher, or spending time selecting a senior member of staff to whom to delegate contact with the researcher. The person who will be the contact with the researcher will be the one who, after the first flush of enthusiasm, will have to persuade stressed, busy teachers that this is a good use of their time. Try at the stage of writing the proposal to calculate how much of each teacher's time will be needed and how much of the contact teacher's time will be involved. Are there jobs to be done that do not require a teacher but can be done by office staff? If this is the case it must be made clear how this will be arranged and whether the time will be paid for. This is particularly important if the proposal includes mailing questionnaires to a cohort of the pupils' parents.

In connection with this, it is necessary to consider what information the schools are at liberty to give us. In a recent project, written into the proposal was that questionnaires should be sent to every pupil's home for the parents to complete. When the schools were identified and the addresses of pupils were requested only 3 schools out of 48 felt sufficient trust in the researchers to provide these lists. Other schools understandably refused on ethical grounds. This immediately meant that the budget was under threat as serialised letters had to be sent to each school and administrative staff paid to address them and post them.

Some schools sent bills for postage, others gave out the letters to pupils as they left at the end of the day. In the proposal it was stressed that letters were to be sent direct to parents since (a) they were more likely to be delivered, and (b) the parents would be confident that the information they provided was not for the school. A freepost envelope was in each. In some schools that gave out the letters pupils were told to bring the letters in to be posted from school so that they could be ticked off a list. Although in these cases the teachers felt that they were being helpful they had invalidated the original proposal that the parent questionnaires were strictly between the research organisation and the parents. With hindsight those who wrote the proposal now realise that it was unrealistic to expect the schools to hand out addresses of pupils. We also now realise that the senior management of some schools like to feel that they have control over any activity in their schools.

The proposal also instructed that any parents who did not return question-naires after 10 days would be sent another, and if this was not returned after 10 days a third and final questionnaire would be sent. Because of pressure of other events, few schools had even sent out the initial questionnaires within 10 days. Some first mailings were found in a store cupboard two months later. Many questionnaires never reached the parents as heads were eager to save us money by giving them to the children.

The sending of parent questionnaires and then teacher questionnaires was simply the preliminary stage of the research. The main part was identifying 500 children throughout England for detailed case studies. Not only was this held up by the tardiness of the parents' questionnaire returns, but also by the reluctance of many of the teachers to complete their questionnaires. This was not purely because of an over-ambitious proposal, but because many heads and other contact staff had not informed the teachers of the cohort of students identified that they would be involved in this. As proposed, in order that teachers would see this as something they were doing for us and not for their heads, their questionnaires were sent directly to them personally (at the school address), with a freepost envelope in which to return them. For many teachers this file of work came to them like a bolt out of the blue. The headteacher had agreed to the research and the secretary had either sent out the letters or given them to teachers to distribute at home time. We were in danger of losing most of our schools and, unfortunately, we did lose several where we had obtained good returns from parents.

There were a number of schools that, when approached, explained that they could not consider the research until they had consulted staff. Of these, less than half agreed to be participants. However, those who had the agreement of the whole staff have stayed with the project.

In another proposal it was intended to interview the head, the Special Needs Coordinator, a volunteer teacher, a parent and a statemented child from each of nine high schools. One of the schools had hoped to take part, but since the proposal had included the headteacher, and she genuinely did not have the time to be interviewed, just eight schools were used. Since this was a well-established girls' school that had just taken in its first intake of boys, as it became co-educational, perhaps staff feelings about support for special needs in school would have been influenced by their new experience. With hindsight I now think that, as long as I had the good will of the headteacher, the inclusion of this school would have provided very useful data.

During the course of this research project, it became obvious that much of the relevant information was with the part-time teachers who supported individual children in the classrooms. In order to obtain as much information as possible these teachers were also included. They were interviewed separately and they also allowed a lively discussion, which was part of an INSET (in-service training) course run by the author, to be recorded. This was not in the proposal but was a valid area of focus when looking at all aspects of special needs support in the classroom. Without the inclusion of these teachers, the identification of indicators of successful support for special needs in secondary schools would have lacked an important dimension (Lovey 1995).

Since the proposal is usually linked to the funding of the project, and schools are becoming more and more like businesses, it is important to consider what we can offer in return for a school's participation. For some schools it is enough to know that they are part of a project that might influence the local authority, or the government in an aspect which is dear to them. Nevertheless, they need reassurance that the project will not actually cost them anything. This is why it is important, when writing a project which entails interviewing teachers, to allow funds for supply cover in the budget, and to bear in mind that although the teacher will receive a sum according to their point on the pay-spine, some schools will add on national insurance and superannuation. One authority only allowed us to contact their teachers if we were willing to offer supply cover. This proviso was made after the project had had funding granted that did not allow for this amount of supply cover. Fortunately, only 4 of the 13 schools asked for supply cover.

Others wish to be assured that they will receive a copy of the final report. Remember, especially if your research is part of a course of study, rather than a funded project, printing out and mailing even eight copies of a report can add considerably to expenses. Where it is a large, widespread project, this will need specific funding, and so will interim newsletters sent to participants to sustain the original interest.

When writing the proposal it is important to bear in mind:

♦ How much will this cost?
♦ Is all this achievable in the time allowed, given that this is a priority for the researcher but will not be for the school?
♦ Is information being requested that schools are uneasy about providing?
♦ Are the teachers, as well as the headteacher, or research contact, aware of their role in this project?
♦ Is the outcome of this research going to add to present knowledge of the subject in a significant way?

A certain flexibility can be accommodated in most research projects but it is important that the proposal is carefully enough written in the first place for a clear focus to be maintained.

The school year

Both when writing the proposal and recruiting the schools, it is important to understand the impact that the school year can have on research. If you are doing a study that will last over a year chose your cohort of pupils carefully. Remember that not only for Year 11 students, but also for pupils at 7, 11 and 14 there is a period of the summer term which is a 'no go' area. This cuts down considerably the number of weeks when data can be collected.

Christmas festivities in primary schools, and teacher fatigue as they approach the end of the longest term in the year, can hamper research activity in schools during December. Make sure that you have a list of the holiday dates for all the authorities with whom you are working. There is a handful of authorities that have very different holidays from most. It is important that researchers do not bank on being able to work in schools at the very end of term or during school holiday periods. Since we 'feed' off the schools, any work we do must be convenient to the staff concerned.

Recruiting the schools

Before recruiting the schools to take part in the project it is important to have a list of criteria by which to select the schools you are going to approach. Having selected the schools you are going to approach, bear in mind that at least half of them might not want to take part. As teacher-in-charge of what was then known as a disruptive unit in the late 1970s, I was flattered when researchers sent questionnaires and asked to interview me. By the mid-1980s, I was suffering from research fatigue as more and more people were studying in this field, and I resented giving yet more time to researchers when they never sent me the reports they had promised. There was one university from which I always received a report and a short note of thanks, and postgraduates from that university were still welcome.

Make sure you have a clear idea of how you are going to recruit your school or schools. The first small piece of research I undertook (not one of the three case studies) was an attempt to find out how many students in off-site units wanted to receive accreditation for their learning, what examination bodies provided the opportunity for this accreditation and how important it was to students, their parents and their future employers (Lovey 1991). I recruited the units for my research by looking at the 'posts advertised' section of the *Times Educational Supplement* (*TES*) for three consecutive Fridays. It was at a time when units were being closed to be replaced by outreach teams, and my rationale was that if a unit was advertising for staff to work there, it must be viable and have prospects of staying open in the foreseeable future. I selected my employers from the vacancies page in the local paper. Here the rationale was that if they were advertising for school leavers they must have an opinion on the value of different types of accreditation.

The research on indicators of successful classroom support was for the LEA (local education authority) in which I then worked, so it was done in secondary schools in which I was already involved. This can be difficult as one has to switch from colleague to researcher, and it is difficult to interview without acknowledging prior knowledge of what is important in that school.

In my research on the fate of young people excluded from school during Key Stage 4 (Lovey et al. 1993), an initial questionnaire was sent to each local authority, and clusters of authorities were selected for case studies. Selecting a couple of authorities which were near together often led to exploring facilities in neighbouring authorities. There were a number of really exciting initiatives in authorities from which replies had not been sent. The network of professionals involved with excluded 14–16 year olds nearly always informed us of other instances of successful, empowering practice. Although we had started with the criterion of studying, in detail, resources described to us by education officers who returned our questionnaires, other places we explored fulfilled the criteria for establishments that engaged young people who were alienated from mainstream education. In research on exclusion from school there is now a large network of committed professionals, and it is important to access this network if researching in this field. Often it is only after embarking on the research project that one learns about vital networks engaged in the researcher's area. Similar networks exist for, among others, those studying various genetic disorders and for the provision and understanding of the specific needs of gifted children.

For another project it was necessary to ensure that a cross-section of schools in six authorities throughout England were recruited. It was decided to recruit two primary schools and one secondary school that were in the top 25 per cent of schools in the league tables, and also had low incidence of free school meals, and the same set of schools from the middle of the league tables with average free school meals, and again from the bottom 25 per cent in the league tables and with above average free school meals. A short list of schools was drawn up with the use of league tables published in the press and freely available. Obtaining data of school meals proved a little more difficult as some local education authority officers were unsure why we wanted these tables, especially as some had recently put their school meals' provision out to private tender. With hindsight, we realised a prior letter describing the project might have been helpful. Although there is value in telephoning to solicit support for a project, it is advisable to refer to a letter that is in the post, which will have details of the project. The timing of the phone call is then important. It is perhaps better to risk phoning before the letter has arrived than phoning so long after dispatching the letter that it is lost in a pile.

Once a cluster of schools in each category had been identified from league tables and free school meal data, the Internet was used to help with the final selection of nine schools in each authority plus nine reserve schools in case the identified school refused to become involved. The DfEE league table data on the Internet was invaluable since it not only gave us statistics such as school size, but also the addresses and phone numbers of the headteachers. Since both of the preferred schools in each category and the reserve school often refused to participate, it was useful to have school meal data and easy access to the Internet to identify further schools in our chosen authorities.

Because it was written into the proposal, which had received outside funding, that the cross-section of schools would be co-educational, when all the mixed schools in one category in one of the authorities refused to take part, two parallel single sex schools were recruited. In one category the only headteacher initially willing to take part had too few pupils of the targeted age group, but was really enthusiastic. He recruited another small school nearby and they worked as one school. They both fulfilled the criteria for the category, and had, in any case, often shared resources. In another category, two schools in the process of combining, but at the time on two adjacent sites, were recruited as one school. This was justified because otherwise there would have been an important section of the school population that would not have been represented in the project.

When you are recruiting schools you will need to understand the power of the school secretary. She, or occasionally he, will almost always be your first contact in the school. Even though it is vital to communicate with the head, or the member of staff delegated by the head as the liaison between the school and researcher, time spent cultivating the school secretary is time well spent. If there is a rapport between the secretary and the researcher, messages will not be forgotten and it will sometimes be possible to be put through to the head on the first attempt. He or she will be an important ally.

During the last 15 years the spotlight has been on education. Some schools have been named, blamed and shamed, leaving the staff feeling totally disempowered, and many of the pupils and their families with a feeling of disappointment, bewilderment and sorrow. There are a few headteachers of such schools who still have confidence in their school and their staff and might initially regard an invitation to be part of a research project as affirmation that the school can survive. A school like this might be very interesting and rewarding for a short-term project, but there is a risk that the head will not be pleased with feedback and might end up feeling betrayed by the researcher as well. If you are recruiting schools in a region with which you are not familiar, you might be unaware that a school you are recruiting is earmarked for closure. If you have chosen your school from a list provided by the local authority the staff there might see your involve-ment as a sign that the closure might not take place. It is difficult to avoid being drawn into the situation in a school where the staff are in a state of anxiety for their future and will use the presence of a researcher as another straw to cling to.

If you have chosen your schools from a local authority list, either provided for you by the LEA or from the Internet, make sure you know about any schools which are to be merged or closed. Unless you are exploring the effect of school closure on a community, avoid these schools.

When preparing to do research on an aspect of the curriculum in off-site areas, during a period of great change, I selected the units for preliminary contact from those who were advertising in the *TES* for new staff during a 3-week period in April. My rationale was that units who were advertising for permanent staff to start in September must have a fair idea that the unit would last at least until the end of the next school year. This was also a way of ensuring it was a fairly random selection that covered all areas of the country. It also meant that the researcher had no preconceptions about the unit and its staff.

Working with schools

The schools have been recruited and the initial stages are underway. Do the schools really know exactly the extent of their commitment? In the enthusiasm to recruit schools, the researchers on one project did not always stress to the headteacher that there were several distinct parts to this research. Naturally, every establishment approached had received a letter with an account of the complete demands of the participating schools. By the time the second part of the survey was sent to schools, some schools had forgotten their original commitment; for some, staffing had changed; inevitably, a number were preparing for, undergoing, or recovering from OFSTED inspections. Researchers have to realise that their priorities are often very low on the school's list of priorities.

It is very important that when arranging to observe or interview teachers, the researcher can be sensitive to the needs of the teacher. Some teachers are happy for the researcher to arrive in the classroom with them. Others might like to have the class settled first and arrange a time for the researcher to arrive, or send a child to collect the researcher. Once the observations have been arranged it is important that none of this valuable time is lost. Observing a class as a researcher can be difficulty for many teachers-turned-researchers, since it is difficult to suppress prior assumptions and make the scene of the research exotic enough to be able to concentrate on a classroom observation as intently as one might do in a less familiar place. Sanger explains his first experiences of classroom observation thus:

> It was not until 1980, thirty-seven years after being born, that I first realised there was a difference between seeing and observing. All those years I had found my way round with unconscious lack of precision, only observing when I needed to remember a route, or a page for an exam, or the face of someone who might turn out to be important to me.

(Sanger 1996: 1)

However, perhaps the difficulty faced in researching a situation in which the researcher was formerly a player might be compensated for by the fact that as a former teacher one understands the pressures under which teachers work. From this privileged position it is important to be sensitive in acknowledging that your research agenda might run counter to how the school wishes to be perceived. Even good schools have often not escaped completely unscathed as competition has been encouraged among schools, and a reputation for excellence in catering for the needs of all children, including those with very distinct special needs, can be regarded as a death knell for some headteachers. When researching indicators of effective support for special needs in mainstream classrooms one head, with an exceptionally good record in this area, was very concerned that his school should not be identifiable.

Because it has been a time of great change, there has been little difficulty in finding an area of the curriculum, academic or pastoral, to research. In some schools children will simply turn to the stranger in the classroom and ask whether he or she is a student or a researcher. However, for some classes the researcher will cause some disruption initially. It is very important to agree how you will be introduced to the class, or indeed whether you will be introduced or whether you will be yet another visitor in the classroom. The researcher will have a task to fulfil, which has been explained to the staff at the school. Therefore, it is important to negotiate a position in the classroom where it is possible to carry out this task. Sometimes teachers will invite you to join in with the activity. This might be an excellent way to obtain some data, but collection of other data might be utterly dependent on careful observation, which would be impossible for a participant. It might be that this kind of observation cannot be achieved until the children are used to you being there. It is difficult to know what effect the researcher has on a class. After one lesson a teacher told me that my presence had made a difference. Since the class had been lively I was about to apologise, when she said that they were so good, they must have thought I was an inspector!

An important skill needed when working in schools is to recognise the priorities of the staff within them while still keeping the focus of the original research. With the best will in the world teachers will invite you to spend time exploring areas that are not relevant to the research. If time in school is limited it is important to be able to politely decline the invitation whilst not dismissing the subject. However, if you have time, admiring a display that a teacher has spent hours preparing for an open day, or attending a school play that is on during your period of researching will gain good will from the staff involved. It might give you further insights into the area of curriculum, the children or the staff you are researching, but it may well just be a way of giving a little bit back to those on whom you rely to provide you with data. Having said this, unless you are doing participant research (Mac an Ghail 1991), make sure that you do not become so embroiled in the life of the school that it affects your relationship with the data, which must remain your priority.

It is very difficult for researchers who have been, or maybe still are, teachers to come to a new research project without preconceptions of how the schools will function. Since all of us have at some time been at school, all of us carry with us some internalised memories of what a school is and how it works. Again, this is where it is important that you are totally committed to the focus of the research as stated in the proposal. There will be all kinds of distractions, especially when classroom observations start and it might be difficult not to become distracted by areas outside the original scope of the research.

Confidentiality

One of the first things to do when embarking on school research is to decide the codes for the schools. This is particularly important if you work in an institution where there are a number of in-service courses for teachers. On a recent project we decided to give all our schools the names of authors. To make this easy to remember it was originally decided to use an author whose name began with the fifth letter of the school's name. However, it was later agreed to let the schools select their own author. Since this was a project where the teachers were partners in the research, this was the right action. However, in another research project, the researchers used the names of trees that began with the third letter of the schools' name. When the research was written up there was a small, unimportant detail inserted in each case study so that no one could positively identify the units.

If the researcher becomes used to always using the pseudonym of the school there is no risk of a visiting teacher, who overhears conversation between researchers in the refectory, identifying the school being discussed. When we were doing research with teachers we were careful not to disclose their pseudonyms to the other schools in the project. However, in a meeting, the heads and other coordinators decided to do this themselves. This had to be their decision, not ours.

The situation where researchers reach the parents of pupils through the school can be a difficult one. Very few schools would entrust the addresses of pupils to us so we had to send letters through the school. The follow up was a similar questionnaire sent to all teachers. Initially the plan was to ask only for details about those whose parents had returned questionnaires. However, since some schools were putting pressure on pupils to persuade their parents to return the questionnaires, it would have been a breach of faith to send a list to the school. There had been the opportunity for parents to refuse and a few did. There was unease about giving this information to the school as, again, it could be prejudicial to future dealings between the school and the parent. In the end, we simply did not include a questionnaire for that child.

At the second phase further questionnaires were sent out to parents whose children had scored highly on a subscale that suggested they might have a behavioural disorder. Again the school was asked to address and send sealed and stamped letters to a small number of children. Although teachers had not been told why these children had been singled out, there was a fair chance they would have some idea. However, parents were given the opportunity not to take part, and teachers were asked to give information on all children. Confidentiality had been kept as far as it could be if a certain group of children were going to be identified and studied. Without this kind of research, resources could be wasted providing the wrong kind of support for these children and their families.

Rewarding the schools

For every school that will join in with research because the staff believe in the intrinsic value of it, there seems to be one where the staff will ask what they will 'get out of it'. In some cases, this might be the opportunity to participate in the research, and sometimes even have this work accredited as part of an ongoing professional development course. Others will be pleased to receive a report when the research is finished. If this has been promised, it should be a point of honour to deliver it, as any research done in a school will involve sacrifices made by teachers. Increasingly heads are beginning to point out the time that filling in questionnaires, etc. will take their staff, and are reluctant to ask them to do this in their own time.

During a recent research project, our contact in one of the LEAs insisted that schools in that area should be offered a day's supply cover for anything the teachers had to do. In the event not all claimed this, but a few schools in another authority, at school level, made this a condition of their continued involvement in a research project. This had not been written into the proposal. Provision had been made to give schools a token for the school library and a small token for each member of staff filling in tick-lists. There was a danger that the few schools that had insisted on supply cover would use up the money earmarked for the 'gifts'. At the time of writing this has still not been resolved.

Because of the way schools are funded, and in recognition of the many stresses on teachers, it is wise to write into the original proposal the means to compensate teachers for their time. In another project a head suggested a 'couple of bottles of wine' for each of his staff. The bill was £150, but since good data had already been collected from the school, it was important that other aspects should be covered if the data were to be useful in the context of the whole project. In two of these projects there has been concern that those who have responded without payment will hear of colleagues whose time has been paid for. This underlines the necessity to write provision for this into the original proposal. When this is done, bear in mind not only the daily supply rate for a teacher who has taught for nine years or more, but also the percentage that must be added to this for national insurance and superannuation. If this is passed through the education office the bill can be nearly 30 per cent higher.

Dissemination of findings

An important task, when the research is done, is the dissemination. Decisions have to be made as to how this is to be done and to whom. If the funding has come from an outside body there might be little choice about the dissemination. In this case it is important to remember that, as a researcher, you have worked for the funding agent, via the university, and the sponsor's logo will have been on all correspondence, newsletters and reports, as well, in some cases, as the funding serial number.

It is very important to know what you may do with research that has been funded externally. If the project is running short of money as it nears its end and there is enough information to hold a conference, this is a possibility, as long as the funders agree. The conference can serve to disseminate the work you are doing and also bring in those people who may ultimately use your research. You have already spent some months absorbing the thoughts and words of the teachers and pupils participating in the study. The conference, with its workshops and social times will add to the insights that have already been gained in the field.

In one research project where a team in each school had researched alongside the university researchers, workshops were run by each team, and led by the teachers. In five out of the six cases it was clear that both groups of researchers were agreed in both the aims of the research and the findings so far. However, it was possible to understand why the sixth project had not proceeded as planned. The two groups had very different agendas and expectations. After the conference it was possible to tackle this and decide the way ahead.

The newsletter, the research article in the paper and the conference can be done whilst the research is still very 'live'. The book or books from the research will take much longer, as will papers in referenced journals. It is when you have convinced a publisher that you have something to say that has not been said before and you have signed the contract to deliver a manuscript in eight or nine months time that you are so glad that you still have all the notes that you made from the first day onwards. It is important to jot everything down from the very beginning, including phone calls you make to schools, even if at the time they seem of little importance. It is later that this kind of information may explain why the results from one school seem to differ from those from another similar school. Research peers will often be as interested in the process as in the theoretical outcomes.

Conclusion

The fact that we have all spent a significant part of our lives in school might well make this a more difficult area to research. Those whose experience is limited to their days as a pupil might still feel that their experience of school is typical of all schools. Those who come to research from a career in the classroom may, initially, find it difficult to regard the environment with the detachment necessary to explore in a sharply focused manner.

Despite the 'research fatigue' suffered by some schools, it is still possible to find schools that welcome the opportunity to be part of a well-conceived research project, especially if they can see the advantages of the possible outcomes of the study. However, it is important to bear in mind that each time a teacher agrees to fill in a questionnaire, they are giving us a gift of their time and their knowledge of the children they teach, or the way in which they teach; when they allow us to interview them they are giving us a gift of a part of themselves. For this reason we must do our best to make it a rewarding experience for the school too. It is easy to depart when the data are collected and forget that we have made ourselves a brief part of the history of that school and that they will hope to see some evidence of the part they played in our project. If they have been our partners in the planning of the research and the collecting of the data, then they must be involved in some of the dissemination.

Educational research is a rich and varied field in which to work. It is an ever-changing world which reflects political and sociological changes and developments. Perhaps the only reward that we can tentatively offer teachers is the knowledge that through research changes in policy might eventually be underpinned by evidence from the 'chalk face'.

References and further reading

Limerick, B., Burgess-Limerick, T. and Grace, M. (1997) The politics of interviewing, power relations and accepting the gift. *International Journal of Qualitative Studies in Education*, 9(4): 449–60.

Lovey, J. (1991) The dilemma of entering disruptive and disaffected adolescents for external examinations. *Maladjustment and Therapeutic Education*, 9(2): 73–82.

Lovey, J. Docking, J. and Evans, R. (1993) *Exclusion from School: Provision for Disaffection in Key Stage 4*. London: David Fulton.

Lovey, J. (1995) *Supporting Special Needs in Secondary School Classrooms*. London: David Fulton.

Mac an Ghaill, M. (1991) Young, gifted and black: methodological reflections of a teacher researcher. In G. Walford *Doing Educational Research*. London: Routledge.

Sanger, J. (1996) The Complete Observer; A Field Research Guide To Observation. London: Falmer Press.

Index